SON OF MY LAND

Copyright © 2013 by Sagi Melamed
All rights reserved.

ISBN: 1-4840-1709-9
ISBN-13: 978-1-4840-1709-8
Library of Congress Control Number: 2013906711
CreateSpace Independent Publishing Platform
North Charleston, South Carolina

For Betsy, my wife. Through your eyes Israel looks tenfold better, and my promise to you I long to keep.

SON OF MY LAND

SAGI MELAMED

WHAT THEY SAY ABOUT SON OF MY LAND:

"An insightful book about Israel, *Son of My Land* reveals the emotions and dreams of the people who live in this remarkable country. May God forever bless Israel."

Robert L. Shook, *New York Times* bestselling author, Columbus, USA

"Son of My Land, an extraordinary perspective of humanity and of Israel by Sagi Melamed—thought-provoking, sobering, yet delicate and heart-warming!"

Robert Zarnegin, Beverly Hills, USA

"Sagi Melamed is truly a son of Israel, with an advanced degree from Harvard University and an American wife. That is why his current observations of life in Israel, his superb insights into the mentality and psyche of the Israeli people, make for compelling reading and offer so much for our reflective thinking."

Alan Schonberg, chairman, Ohio-Israel Chamber of Commerce, Cleveland, USA

"Optimism, optimism in Zionism, optimism in Israel, and optimism in the Israeli people is the constant thread in the fabric of Sagi Melamed's essays, gathered together in *Son of My Land*. When spirits flag, when skepticism and cynicism appear to be appropriate, take up a Melamed essay. Strength, heart, and enthusiasm return. We know that the Jewish people have created something remarkable, modern Israel, and we are proud to be a part of it and a companion of Sagi."

S. Lee Kohrman, Cleveland, USA

"The realization that Israel's existence as an independent state isn't a foregone conclusion…drives Sagi to prose that cries out to be heard…that often smolders in anger but is always filled with great love."

Rabbi Dr. Benjamin Lau, Jerusalem, Israel

"Sagi Melamed enjoys a remarkable ability to see greatness in small events and the extraordinary in daily life.

He has a wonderful ability to pinpoint current issues and bring them to the reader wrapped in descriptions and experiences of daily life in Israel, which makes it very easy to understand at the same time as it reveals the vibrant, mixed, and lively society in Israel with all its challenges, both internal and external."

Per-Åke Elisson, pastor, Kristet Center-Örebro, Sweden

"Sagi Melamed, a sabra and an observant Jew, writes with deep compassion and respect for all the peoples living in the land of Israel. His insights into everyday family life, internal strife, and international conflicts enrich a reader's knowledge of current events and offer a vision of hope for the future."

Sheila and Bob Friedland, White Plains, New York, USA

"When you read Sagi Melamed's *Son of My Land*, you will want to visit this remarkable country of Israel. It certainly kindled that desire in me! Thank you, Sagi, for giving us the opportunity and privilege to better understand these wonderful people of your beautiful land."

David Steward, chairman, World Wide Technology, St. Louis, USA

"*Son of My Land* is a series of short essays and vignettes by an Israeli-raised and Harvard-educated Jewish father of four who seeks justice, peace, and opportunity for all in his homeland.

In addition to his own insights and philosophy, what makes this book both fun and fascinating to read are the contrasting views of Sagi's wide variety of friends and acquaintances. They range from an ultra-orthodox Jew, who wants to see the Israeli state fail so that the coming Messiah can reclaim it, to the young Palestinian mother who is much more worried about the oppression she has from her own family. Sagi brings all these people to life, allowing us to see modern-day Israel through different prisms."

Larry Smith, Boston, USA

"Sagi is a master storyteller, captivating readers with his in-depth insights into human nature and the struggles of Israel and its people. He possesses an amazing knowledge of the Israeli culture and effortlessly transports the reader into his world."

Aliki and Peter Rzepka, Cleveland, USA

TABLE OF CONTENTS

Foreword i

Welcome to First Grade—What Kind
of Israel Is Sivan Growing Up In?................................... 1

A Rainbow over the Galilee 11

A Hidden Cave 15

The Look in Their Eyes 21

A Nuclear Iran—The Real Big Question 27

Every Hebrew Soldier Must Know................................. 31

On Promises and Cakes 35

On Entering and Exiting 41

Hope 47

Not What We Were Promised... 51

What Connects Us? 55

Fears.. 63

From a Distance Everything Is Nearer.......................... 71

Sabras.. 75

Each Side Manages to Convince Me That the
Other Side Is Right 81

Street Cat 87

Peace Duty 93

Can Might and Peace Live Together? 97

Exodus 103

You're Also Right 111

For We Held Peace in Our Hands 115

Immigrants 117

The Zionist Soul... 121

Solidarity... 125

While Facing the Great Synagogue of Budapest........................ 129

Holocaust? Remind Me Please… 133

So Much Can Be Learned from Children 137

Tournament of War 141

So, What Should We Do?... 145

Some Say That Contemporary Israel Is Europe
of the 1930s Era.. 155

On the Knife... 159

Connected?.. 165

Everything Is Political 171

From Pioneering Leader to Museum Exhibit 175

Modesty 181

Money or Ideas? 185

Daily Newspaper 191

To Be an Officer 195

Son of a Kibbutz—Assets and Liabilities 201

Freedom of the Spirit 209

Strudel Doesn't Cross Borders 213

From Berlin to MTV 219

A King 223

Occupy… 229

Yes, She Can! 235

Dirt 239

And Show Deference 245

They Don't Make This Kind of People Anymore 251

Mah Yihiyeh? 255

Gam ve Gam 259

Being Chosen Carries Obligations 263

FOREWORD

As the sound of buckling seatbelts is heard, the descent toward Ben-Gurion Airport begins, and the aircraft emerges from behind the clouds, revealing a narrow strip of sandy beach below. The thin, white ripple of foam that connects land and sea heralds our eager return: small but brazen and feisty. I have arrived. I'm home.

I was born and raised on a kibbutz, nursed on the stories of the Palmach and the Haganah, Zionist youth movements, and the Holocaust. I was told of the barren wilderness, of the pioneers who dried up the swamps, and of their heroic triumph over the Land of Israel.

Following high school, I volunteered for a year of community service as a kibbutz youth leader, after which I started my military service. It was during this time that my eyes were opened to a diverse Israeli population—urban, religious, and minority.

I did my military service from 1984 to 1988, in the throes of the first intifada. While serving as a platoon commander, I felt budding concern and angst about the path our country was choosing to take and for its future. Upon the completion of four years of military service and my release from the army, I crossed the threshold back into the real world. I acquired an education, wove an international network of friends and colleagues, and was exposed to different points of view. Only when I began raising my own family did the disquiet and concern intensify.

I have heard Shimon Peres claim that an optimist and a pessimist arrive at the same destination; however, the optimist is the one who will have enjoyed the journey. This is an astute observation and one that I reflect on often. For years I was under the impression that perhaps my fears about Israel's destiny stemmed from my own personality—my own "stuff," as it were. However, over time, I simply became more and more preoccupied with thoughts about where we are heading. A lucid look at reality justified the feeling that my concerns were not completely unfounded.

When I was in kindergarten, the teacher, on Independence Day, put up a string of plastic flags on which Israeli army generals were represented. This was the period between the Six-Day War and the Yom Kippur War; Israel was strong, bold, and invincible. It was also indisputable that "the guys in control" knew what needed to be done. There were people to trust—or so we thought. Since then, Israel has sobered. Flags of generals do not decorate kindergartens on Independence Day, and it is more likely that kids will recognize the "heroes" on "Big Brother" rather than the officers of the IDF. Ostensibly, this is a positive turn of events. We desire to be like other nations, unencumbered by war and able to enjoy harmless frivolities, to be mesmerized by the TV series "Survival" instead of fighting for our own survival.

Yet we cannot rest on our laurels; the threat of being annihilated is constant, and it is all too clear that our children will have to raise their swords just as we did. Perhaps my doubts are exacerbated by the fact that my first-born son is about to enlist in the military. Talk of classification and assessment exams, combat units, conscription dates, and all sorts of army jargon brings me back thirty years. It seems only a moment ago that it was I who was doing my preliminary training before my service. I had dreamt of a meaningful military experience; I aspired to be an officer and to be a hero. The unrequited promise of the past generations—that my grandfather promised my father, and my father promised me, and I promised my own son—has not been fulfilled for four generations. My son Guy is the fourth generation of Melameds on his way to the front. I regard this with deep anguish.

My generation, those of us who were born between Israel's two great wars, the one that induced intoxicating power and grandeur and the other, from which we have sobered, are the ones who now carry the responsibility. There is no longer anyone to turn to, no more heroes to hold in esteem—no one who understands more and knows better, no one who knows exactly what to do. It is clear that those people no longer exist, or perhaps they never did. In the Book of Deuteronomy, *Parashat Nitzavim*, two alternatives are offered: "Behold, I have set before you today life and prosperity, and death and adversity…"

Have we, the residents of the State of Israel, truly chosen life and prosperity?

Yoram Taharlev writes the following lines in his book *The First Kiss*:

Fortunately, there will always be someone more foolish than I.

There will always be someone weaker than I.

There will always be someone who will die before me, and I have nothing to fear as long as that someone is alive.

Contrary to the hero of Taharlev's poem, Israel must always be the strongest, the smartest, and the most just. Truthfully, this is a difficult task. We do not have the freedom of being mediocre, of being almost strong, a little bit smart, or kind of just. We will not be given, nor do we get, a second chance.

Israel is struggling to survive and flourish under almost impossible circumstances, surrounded by adversaries, with almost no natural resources, with narrow and disputable borders, in an impatient, melting-pot society. Looking back less than a hundred years, the State of Israel can be perceived as a miracle. Even the most delusionary dreamers among the founders of the state would have had a hard time conjuring up a picture of our country today: independent, sassy, satiated, and prosperous.

Throughout the years, I have traveled and lived portions of my life outside of Israel. From time to time, I ask myself if I might prefer living in another country, if there were another place where I would like to live. The answer is always an undisputable no.

It is impossible to define my connection to Israel one-dimensionally; it is a weave of memories, tastes, smells, and senses that begins with my grandfather, Manfred Friedlander—who Hebraized his name to Michael *Benartzi* (which means "Son of My Land") when he came to Israel from Germany—and continues with the smell of orange blossoms in the spring, the tranquility of Sabbath eve, the grit of army reserve duty, the Israeli flag waving proudly, the winds of autumn beckoning Rosh Hashanah, pink cyclamen peeking out after the rains, finely chopped salad, the sunrise from the top of

Masada, "Believe it! The day will come" sung on Independence Day, images from the Holocaust, the prayer for the State of Israel, etc., etc. It's hard to say if this is good or bad, but the union that binds me to this tiny, crowded place, situated among Asia, Europe, and Africa, is genuine and irrevocable.

And on this wide-scoped, winding path, among a deep-seated love for Israel, the feeling of ownership and belonging, the pride and satisfaction reaped from what has been achieved here in such a short time under trying conditions, and the anxiety over the welfare, the strength, the morale, and the future of Israel, the following words have been written.

Presented to the State of Israel with love and trepidation,

Sagi Melamed, 2013
Melamed.sagi@gmail.com

WELCOME TO FIRST GRADE - WHAT KIND OF ISRAEL IS SIVAN GROWING UP IN?

September 1, 2010. Sivan, our fourth and youngest child, is about to start first grade. The first day of first grade was always exciting with every one of our kids, but somehow this time it's different.

For weeks leading up to this day, I wasn't able to contain myself, asking over and over, "Sivan, are you as excited as Daddy is?" And each time, with a shy smile, came the inevitable reply: "No." But as the big day drew closer, even Sivan couldn't conceal her anticipation. Suddenly it was hard for her to fall asleep, and she could only doze off with her hand in mine. Her guileless questions revealed fears over leaving behind the known world of no responsibilities to enter a new realm of frameworks, rules, and expectations. "Daddy, what if the teacher tells us what to do, and I don't understand?"

she asks. And, "Daddy, what do babies do when they don't understand what the teacher says?"

We ended up diverting all our excitement into the preparations—a colorful new school shirt, new schoolbag, and taking inventory to confirm its contents: pencil case, notebooks, lunch box. Like soldiers checking their equipment before setting off to battle.

Now, on this big day, I feel like a combination of kindergarten teacher, shepherd, and Olympic trainer. After six years of loving care, ups and downs, leading and trying to keep up, instilling habits and values, hugs and kisses, today I am escorting her down a new road…

In fact, this excitement we are feeling has much to do with our own experience as well—as parents who are now concluding a chapter in their child-rearing lives. No more mornings walking into the kindergarten hand in hand, stealing a minute to assemble the pieces of a puzzle together before setting off to work. No more folding ourselves onto miniature chairs at Hannuka and Purim kindergarten parties.

My thoughts wander beyond my own personal, family experience to the surrounding spheres. There must be so many others, in Jerusalem, Afula, Ramallah, Nazareth, Ariel, Nahalal, and Eilat, who are sharing a similar moment and are as moved as I. Escorting a small child to first grade, with a prayer in their hearts and on their lips, perhaps in different syllables or cadence but essentially the same, to bless, keep, and return these nestlings safely home.

And I wonder if this unique day could somehow be enlisted to explore what we share in common—and combine our efforts to find ways to live together and ensure a more promising and secure future for these first graders, wherever they may be.

Now, the official ceremony opening the school year at the Hoshaya Elementary School. The orderly line of first graders proceeds into the auspices of the school, passing under an outstretched tallit, accompanied by cheerful music and the sniffling of the parents on the sidelines. With my heart aching with pride and joyful tears on my cheeks, I ponder what lies ahead for them—these first graders of 2010. What kind of world will they struggle to understand and study in school?

I start to do my own mental inventory, trying to evaluate what kind of Israel our Sivan will be growing up in. A list of this and that, of one hand and the other.

The Environment—To Squander and to Preserve

As consciousness in the world has risen regarding protecting the environment, in twenty-first-century Israel this subject is very much on the public agenda. At this point there is broad consensus that the nation's dwindling water resources need to be preserved, and new initiatives are addressing the problem. Educational programs explain the importance of environmental issues in the schools, and an entire spectrum of civic organizations has embraced environmental causes. All these should be a cause for optimism.

On the other hand, it is hard to find in the Western world a country as dirty as Israel. On a family vacation this summer in Slovenia, I reveled in the green landscape, the abundant water, the pristine nature. At one point I mentioned to my wife how depressing it is to compare the cleanliness of Slovenia with Israel. In Slovenia you don't see garbage on the streets, trash outside the cities, or construction debris at the entrance to villages.

And, here, I wonder what God thinks when he looks down on us from above about the way that the Jewish people treat the land given them to work and protect. One can barely walk down the street without seeing discarded bottles, plastic bags, and garbage. Someone who never leaves Israel's borders might think that this is the normal and unavoidable state of affairs. It used to be that, in the name of security, neglecting the environment could be excused. "What alternative do we have?" people said. "This isn't Scandinavia."

When my older daughter asked me what continent Israel is located on, a cynical thought crossed my mind that Israel would like to belong to Europe, is actually located in Asia, but behaves like it is in Africa.

Security

Evaluating Israel's security situation in 2010 depends on which color glasses one wears. Through rose-colored glasses, the situation is excellent. A minimal number of recent terrorist attacks, relative quiet on the borders, an enduring peace with Egypt and Jordan, and an IDF that is better prepared than a few years ago.

But for those wearing dark glasses, the situation is awful and getting worse. In fact, things have never been so dangerous: the extreme Islamic fronts are closing in on us in the south (Gaza), the north (Hezbollah), and the east (Iran and maybe even Iraq). The IDF hasn't won a war for forty-three years, a growing percentage of the population doesn't serve in the army, and, worst of all, the terrifying day is approaching when an enemy country that has declared its intention to destroy Israel can press a button and dispatch a nuclear weapon. And in that enemy country, the rational threat of deterrence, which says that if you attack us, we'll hit back harder, doesn't necessarily make an impression on its leaders.

Israel's Standing in the World

Today, Israel has already crossed the line from being a small nation with a lot of chutzpa, watched with admiring amazement by most of the world as it builds a nation with a robust economy and army, to a country that, despite its small size, is considered to be a military powerhouse—covered by the media without any proportion to its relative position in the world and perceived as the neighborhood bully that crushes and oppresses its neighbors/citizens, the helpless Palestinians.

At a recent breakfast meeting I had with the Israeli ambassador to one of the Western European countries, he laid out for me Israel's declining status in that country, his difficulties presenting the Israeli perspective to increasingly antagonistic audiences, and the increasing costs to protect the security of the local Jewish community.

And on the other hand, there are still large and influential sectors in the world, in North and South America, Europe, and Asia, who staunchly support Israel as a country that embodies the vision of the return of the Jewish people to the land of the Bible. The Evangelist Christian community is perhaps the most outstanding among them. There are estimates that the number of Evangelical Christians supporting Israel for religious reasons is 300 million.

And on the third hand, Israel has succeeded over the years to recruit friends from unlikely places. On my last visit to Stockholm, I stopped for a cup of hot chocolate at a small local café. When I looked at the familiar face of the café owner, I asked him where he was from. "From Lebanon," he replied. I answered him (after a moment of hesitation whether it was better to respond **after** he prepared my drink), "*Ahalan bik. Aana min Israil. Nekhna jhiran*" (Arabic for "Greetings. I'm from Israel. We are neighbors"). With a smile, he whispered that he is Christian, from Zakhlata, and that he admires Israel for helping the Christians of Lebanon. To top off his sentiment, he gave me a discount on the bill and added a glass of juice on the house.

All of Israel Brothers

In the middle of the second hundred years of the Zionist enterprise, one hundred years of settlement, and sixty-two years since the establishment of the country, it is still difficult to say that all of Israel is brothers.

On the one hand, the acute differences between Ashkenazi and Sephardic Jews, and between immigrants from one country and another, are slowly being erased. This is mainly due to the passage of time and new generations of native-born Israelis, for whom ethnic differences aren't so significant.

On the other hand, there is always someone who manages to emphasize the differences and create "us" and "them": good religious and bad religious, Ethiopians versus veteran Israelis, settlers opposite North Tel Avivians. In my conversation with a nursing student from the Yezreel Valley College, who immigrated to Israel from Ethiopia at the age of thirteen, he shared with me a wound he was carrying in his heart. I asked him, "In the airplane on the way to Israel from Ethiopia, what did you dream of?" His expression was troubled as he answered me: "In Ethiopia, we were persecuted because we are Jewish. On the plane, I dreamed of arriving to a country where I would be accepted as an equal among equals. But when I arrived, I understood that here, too, I'm different."

G-d Willing

A friend from my community of Hoshaya told me once at the entrance to the synagogue, after he'd finished several exhausting years as a highly positioned public servant: "After I learned how our government works, I understood that there is definitely a God in heaven, otherwise our fate would have long since been sealed."

On the other hand, it's a little scary to think what God must think when he sees what is going on down here. Sometimes, during the Haftorah reading on Shabbat, listening to the words of the prophets denigrating the different sins of the people of Israel and the punishments that were inflicted on the sinners, I think of the corruption, the wrongdoings, and the injustices that we live with day to day, and I tremble in fear.

Making Peace

During the first three decades of the State of Israel, we were surrounded by enemies, a few against many. It was a scary picture, but in the background there was always the dream that one day there would be peace. The day will come, and the next generation won't need to go to war. That was the ultimate promise of every Israeli parent. "My children won't have to fight."

It seems that this dream is receding into the distance. In Israel of 2010, it's hard to find parents who assure their children with promises of peace. Even among those who were considered "the peace camp," pessimism reigns. Most of the population (even though they might not want to say it out loud) believes that we will need to keep our swords at the ready for a long time to come. Even worse, the answer to the question that was once considered taboo, "Will Israel always be living in the neighborhood?" isn't obvious. Surrounded by enemies, losing support in the world, facing a scenario where an enemy dedicated to the country's extermination now has the nuclear ability to do so, Israel's survival in the long term faces a giant question mark.

Who Is the Role Model?

During my childhood on the kibbutz, our national heroes were the pioneers, the farmers, the soldiers, and the government ministers and Knesset members, and also, to a small degree, singers and actors. These figures riveted our attention, and the cream of our youth aspired to be like them.

Today the pioneers belong to history, the farmers are Thai workers, being a high officer isn't such a big deal, and politicians are virtually synonymous with corruption.

On the other hand, a high-tech entrepreneur, tycoon, and this or that celebrity have now become the new national role models. Ostensibly, this is all well and good. Finally we are like other nations, and we can focus on the good life.

But focusing on the good life is a privilege that a country surrounded by enemies from outside, and sometimes even from within, cannot afford. Israel cannot survive if the best of its youth want above all to be rich and famous.

So what does all this leave us with—and in what Israel will Sivan and her classmates grow up?

The short answer is: it's not clear.

The longer answer is: it's not clear to me or to others either.

But What IS Clear?

First of all, I believe what every paratrooper learned in basic training: if we won't support one another, we'll hang, one next to the other. Solidarity, shared agenda, and teamwork are critical for us Israelis.

And second of all, on the first of September 2010, Sivan and hundreds of thousands of other students entered Jewish and Israeli schools, in the free and democratic State of Israel, home to the Jewish people, with a Jewish army, Jewish universities, and Jewish industry and agriculture. A country where (almost) every child has a roof over his or her head, clothes to wear and, food on the table.

And that is definitely a reason to be optimistic.

September 2011

A RAINBOW OVER THE GALILEE

A dense foggy morning. The end-of-winter storm the forecasters promised us had stolen over the Mediterranean coast and was gradually taking over the Israeli skies. Already March—almost Purim—and we thought that winter was already behind us. We'd come to terms with the depressing thought that the scanty amount of precipitation we'd been treated to during the winter of Taf Shin Ayin Aleph was all there would be and that it will have to sustain us through another parched summer. More gardens and lawns will be left to dry out. And the price of water will surely keep rising. The Sea of Galilee will continue to recede from its shores. Coming home from school, our children will recite that we need to save water because Israel is drying up.

And then, suddenly, a genuine storm reached our skies. As if from a foreign land where winters are actually wintery. Booming thunder, inky clouds, driving rain, and gale winds. Darkness spread across the country, painting it in shades of gray and black. The green Galilee lost its color. And then, from out of the rain clouds, smiling and confident, a rainbow appeared, stretching across the Bet Netufa Valley. A perfect arc in brilliant colors.

Six thirty AM, I was on my way to work at the Yezreel Valley College, and, out of the corner of my eye, I saw the rainbow. I immediately pulled over outside the gate to our village and got out of the car, even though the intensifying rain threatened to chase away the last remaining rays of sunshine that were still peeking out from behind the clouds. I took out my cell phone and took a picture of the rainbow. I had a feeling that it was a sign of something, although I wasn't sure what. But over the last two days, I figured it out. The rainbow bridges between pessimism and optimism. Between worry and hope. The rainbow seems to be promising to us and all of humanity, scurrying across the Promised Land, all too often forgetting that there is a reason and power behind it all: I am here. There is hope. Don't despair. The covenant is still intact.

There are many reasons for concern here, at the end of winter Taf Shin Ayin Aleph. Yet there is also hope and promise. This combination, between worry and hope, seems to be expressed in the weather, the environment, and in nature.

On the one hand, it is hard to decide what to worry about most, about the troubles near or far. At home, Israel is getting more crowded, plagued by drought, threatened by economic and social inequities, consensuses that were once unquestioned are now in doubt, verbal and physical violence are spreading in society, and, living within it, there is a frustrated, impatient minority, who understands more and more the power of the weak.

In the surrounding neighborhood, the old order is collapsing like a house of cards practically overnight, and in place of the familiar problems, we may face a whole new and even larger set of problems. Iran continues to arm itself and call for the destruction of Israel. Entrenched dictators may be replaced with new, even worse ones, and peaceful borders could ignite.

The larger world is less and less patient with this little country, with its chutzpa, that is seen, paradoxically, in spite of its small size and history of persecution of its people, as the violent bully of the neighborhood. Recently I heard about bizarre guilt feelings: Germany feels guilty toward the Palestinian people because the Jewish people, who were practically exterminated by the German Nazis seventy years ago, found shelter and a national home in Israel at the expense of the Palestinians. And for this reason the Germans need to support the Palestinians in their struggle against Israel.

Yet on the other hand, there are reasons for hope. The neighboring regimes are changing, and those that replace them could be for the better. Perhaps this actually represents the authentic desire of the neighboring peoples to take their futures into their hands and head in the direction of democracy and freedom.

And among ourselves, in spite of it all, we have innovation, creativity, and many reasons for pride and optimism. Two weeks ago in Eilat there was an annual conference on alternative energy. Thousands of companies and interested parties from around the world came to this Red Sea city. Gilad Maoz, a friend and a leading attorney in this field, told me that the conference is turning into one of the most important events in the industry and that Israel is one of the leading centers for achievement and innovation in alternative energy. They say that after the exodus from Egypt, Moses had to lead the Israelites through the desert for forty years—in search of the only country in the Middle East without oil. So we don't have oil, and barely have water, but sunshine and creative minds we have in spades.

In the Book of Genesis, in the portion of Noah, it is written: "I have set My bow in the cloud, and it shall be for a token of a covenant between Me and the earth." And so, in spite of the troubles, threats, and worries, spring is around the corner, more colorful and exuberant than ever. The mountains and valleys of the Galilee are brilliant green, yellow, pink, and red, carpeted in cyclamens, anemones, and wheat. And while these lines are being written, blessed rains are falling across the country, quenching the parched earth and extending a parting gift from winter before it disappears until next year. And every so often a rainbow appears from between the clouds and reminds us: there is hope. The covenant stands.

March 2011

A HIDDEN CAVE

It is Lag Ba'Omer, and the smoke from countless bonfires still hangs in the air from last night. The skies are gray even though the sun has already risen in the east on a cloudless day. I set out for an early-morning bicycle ride through the fields that surround my community of Hoshaya, riding northwest toward the Bet Netufa Valley. These days, the landscape of the Galilee is in flux, shifting from the rich, deep green of spring to the washed-out yellow of summer. The forest green of the pine trees, the silvery shine of the olive trees, and the soft green of the new cotton plants that are peeking out of the rows of heavy earth fade into the greenish yellow of the drying spring weeds and the dusty gold of the wheat stalks after the harvest.

Heading west from Hoshaya, two runners passed me with a cheerful wave. My friends Danny, a professor of philosophy, and Dubi, a pediatrician. They were both wearing professional running clothes and running shoes and, on their arms, sophisticated running watches. I veered north under the highway, with the large artificial reservoir of the national water carrier to my left, pumping and collecting the little water that is left in the Sea of Galilee before sending it southward.

And then I saw him, prodding a flock of sheep that was slowly gleaning from the remaining stalks in the wheat field. A Bedouin shepherd, walking along in measured steps, a little bent over, wearing long clothes, a plaid flannel shirt, a pair of corduroy pants that had seen better days, and high rubber boots, in no relation to the heat of the day and the season, as if their owner forgot that the winter and its mud were already behind us.

I stopped my bicycle next to him and greeted him: "*A salaam aleikum.*" "*Aleikum a salaam,*" he answered warmly, pleased with the opportunity to speak to another person after spending hours in the company of sheep. We exchanged a series of traditional blessings in Arabic, covering the main topics that are important in life: health, peace, family, and livelihood. As always, I was pleased to practice my Arabic, and as rusty as it is from lack of use, I still enjoy the feel of it coming from my mouth.

I quickly learned that the name of this Bedouin man was Yusuf and that he lives in the neighboring Arab-Bedouin village of Arab-el-Heib. The village is situated directly across from Hoshaya, only about one kilometer away. Yet, despite the geographical proximity, any connection between the people of that village and those of Hoshaya is practically non-existent. The only exception is Zaki, the security guard at the school in Hoshaya. Despite his background, Zaki is entrusted with the peace and security of the parents and children alike. Frequently Zaki's presence confuses the younger schoolchildren, who, out of their Israeli reality, believe that Arab = dangerous person. When I told my youngest daughter that Zaki the guard is Arab, she answered me in innocent alarm, "What, Zaki is Arab? I thought Arabs are bad, and Zaki is supposed to protect us?!"

Without my asking, Yusuf told me that he lives next to an ancient cave carved into the earth of a hill that is visible in the middle of the Bet Netufa Valley—a cave that the teenagers of Hoshaya like to hike to and crawl into. "That cave has been here in the valley since the time of the Jewish revolt over the Romans. The Jews hid out in the cave from the Romans two thousand years ago," Yusuf told me. And just like that, with his words, he connected our casual conversation to the tradition of Lag Ba'Omer.

The previous evening, on Erev Lag b'Omer, I discussed with my four children the origins of the celebration of this holiday. I was curious to see how much they knew. Because even I don't remember all the details of the tradition, I took down from the bookshelf a volume from the encyclopedia of Jewish traditions. After I'd read enough to refresh my memory, I focused on the section that explains about the tradition of lighting a bonfire on Erev L"g b'Omer, that same one that the children of Israel have turned into the main purpose of the holiday, for which they collect wood from the end of Pesach to sit around enormous bonfires throughout the night, eating, telling stories, and playing games.

According to tradition, lighting a bonfire on Lag Ba'Omer has its origins in the Jewish revolt against the Romans, when the sign that it was about to happen was relayed from village to village via bonfires that were lit on hilltops across Yehuda and the Galilee.

I took advantage of the opportunity and asked Yusuf the ultimate question: "What will be?" Even without my specifying what I actually meant by that question, Yusuf understood and directed his answer toward the relations between Jews and Arabs and the longed-for peace that is slipping away from us. The old shepherd's answer began with a declaration that he belongs on the good side of the fence: "Everyone in our village served in the army as trackers, in the border police, and the security forces. We don't have any problems…" After that he elegantly passed the responsibility for the situation to the one who is ultimately accountable. "Everything is in Allah's hands," he declared. "I don't know what will be. Everything is in the hands of heaven."

I parted from Yusuf, and he and his herd continued on their way across the middle of the wheat field. I got back on my bike and pondered over our short conversation as I pedaled back to Hoshaya. The exchange with Yusuf reminded me of a large public organization I used to work for. The atmosphere in that organization at that time was grim because of budget cuts, political conflicts, and uncertainty about the future. In conversations I had with some of the more senior employees, those who had worked in the organization for decades, I always got the feeling that they bent in the wind like reeds, waiting to see which direction the wind would blow and when. Who would rise and who would fall. The daily issues were less worrisome for them. Instead, they focused on the future—their pensions, on life after work. To get to their retirement days in peace, they were careful about what they said, avoiding taking any position that would identify them one way or another. They understood that the boss of today may not even be in the organization tomorrow.

In conversations with Arab-Israelis I sense a similar thing. Not just on the side of politicians and intellectuals but also among the simple people, and mainly the adults among them. Sometimes it seems that the day-to-day problems concern them less, and they look to the long term, to the tomorrow and the day after tomorrow. They relate to the complex mosaic that binds our lives together in Israel from a long-term, historical perspective. They understand, not necessarily because of education or grasp of the details of history, but from the wisdom of life that those in control come and go, particularly when it comes to Israel. They wait, patiently, to see who is the strongest, who will rule, and who has the power today and until when.

Because, for thousands of years, in this small and amazing land that is stuck amid Asia, Europe, and Africa, different leaders and kings have risen and fallen, won and lost, conquered and were conquered. And the State of Israel of today exists for less than one hundred years, and already it is so difficult to control what it has conquered and achieved, and the country is torn asunder by opposing powers and forces from within, and pressured by enemies and haters from outside.

Do Yusuf and those like him understand something that we, the current rulers of this land, don't?

May 2011

THE LOOK IN THEIR EYES

Buried among the many year-end events of 2012, one historical milestone was somewhat overlooked: the "silver anniversary" of the outbreak of the first intifada. I was there, in the heart of that tempest in the winter of 1987, in the refugee camps around Ramallah. We were not prepared for an intifada. We had gone to the Ramallah area for seven days of routine security duty and ended up staying there for three full months. Much has been written, said, and claimed regarding the reasons for the intifada, the influences and the implications of the first Palestinian uprising. As a junior officer, I was not privy to the classified intelligence reports that purported to analyze and predict the way the wind was blowing in the Palestinian street. But I did not need intelligence reports to understand that something drastic changed during that period. Right in front of me I saw the look in the eyes of the people in the narrow streets of the neglected refugee camps. The eyes are the window of the soul, and the stares that were directed at us by the inhabitants of the Palestinian refugee camps expressed the dramatic turning point that took place that winter. During my first three years of army service, before the first intifada, I had been in Judea and Samaria several times for routine security duty. These security duties mainly involved foot and motor patrols in and around the refugee camps and major cities, such as Ramallah. A regular patrol consisted of three or four soldiers and a commander. The most serious incidents during that time involved anti-Israel graffiti or pro-Arafat flyers and sometimes the PLO flag being flown from the electricity wires. But the eyes of the Palestinian residents were always downcast. Frightened. Evasive. Ashamed. When they saw the IDF patrol, children would run away, mothers would bring their children inside, teenage boys would vanish. We soldiers would walk without concern or fear, in control of the territory and the people.

In contrast, when the intifada broke out, the look that was cast our way by Palestinian eyes was different. They looked us straight in the face. The people stood their ground. Lips were pursed. Pride was evident on faces. Children no longer ran away but hurled stones and curses. Women did not call their children inside like chickens afraid of the big, bad wolf but joined their children and took an active part in the mass demonstrations. The youth led the riots, throwing rocks and blocking streets, planting metal spikes to puncture the tires of the military vehicles, and later on even shooting at the soldiers.

Blocking the roads showed the extent to which the Palestinian masses were involved in the popular uprising. Our daily routine consisted of motor patrols along the roads that wound between the small villages in the vicinity of Ramallah. When we drove back along the same road we had travelled just a short time before, we could see from afar the pillars of black smoke. As we got closer to the village, we would find that the road was blocked with burning tires and hundreds of rocks, some of them so heavy that it would have taken the combined efforts of several people to move them into place. It was clear that the entire village had participated in blocking the road.

Thus we had the Palestinians, with the outbreak of the popular uprising, discovering their lost pride, while on the other side many soldiers of the Israel Defense Forces were struggling with the basic values with which they had been raised.

I went into the army as a graduate from the kibbutz educational system and having been a counselor in the kibbutz youth movement. I was brought up on the stories of the Warsaw Ghetto uprising, the fighters of the Hagana, and the heroes of the Palmach. They were my lullabies and my guiding light. In the calculus of the few versus the many, I knew that we were the few, the brave, the resourceful. And, above all, that we had right on our side.

But suddenly it was no longer so obvious who were the good guys and who the bad guys. It was clear who were the few, who the resourceful, who the unarmed—and this time it was not us. I remember one significant moment during a foot patrol when I suddenly noticed a paper arrow stuck into the back of the bulletproof vest of one of my soldiers. It was an arrow made of rolled-up paper, like those we used to make as children to shoot out of plastic tubes that we called tfu-tfu. These paper arrows were our main weapon when we played at being soldiers in the cotton barns on the kibbutz. Except this time, a sharp metal pin was attached to the end of the paper arrow, and it was stuck in the back of a real soldier. My soldier. An Israeli soldier.

The declaration of the State of Palestine on the historically significant date of the twenty-ninth of November 2012 came twenty-five years after the outbreak of the first intifada. Much has happened in our neighborhood during that quarter of a century. The Oslo peace process of the middle of the 1990s brought the spirit of hope into the region. Despite the arguments about the long-term value of the Oslo process, there can be no argument about the historical facts: in the middle of the 1990s, Israeli embassies opened up in Arab capitals, and representatives from Arab and others countries came to Israel for the first time, foreign investment in Israel blossomed, and there was the feeling that peace was indeed on the way. True, the price was heavy and accompanied with labor pains, but nevertheless it was coming.

But after Oslo came another intifada and disengagement from Gaza, one violent confrontation and then another, and peace plans and their rejections, and declarations and their non-implementation. Sadly and frustratingly, the raised look and straightened shoulders of the Palestinians that I saw twenty-five years ago did not bring with it political wisdom, or the ability to reach compromises, or to prefer the good of the people over grabbing and clinging to power. Without minimizing the part Israel played in the failure of the peace process, it seems to me that the Palestinians are not blessed with leaders who combine strength, patience, long-term vision, and wisdom, qualities that brought the Jewish people to the historic declaration of a Jewish state on November 29, 1947.

The tragedy of the Palestinians is also—and perhaps even more so—the tragedy of the Israelis. What would still have been possible twenty-five years ago seems impossible today. Paradoxically, what now unites the majority of Israelis and Palestinians is, on the one hand, a theoretical willingness for painful compromise as long as the compromise is fair, honorable, wise, and stable but, on the other hand, a loss of hope and belief that it is possible to achieve such compromise in the foreseeable future.

December 2012

A NUCLEAR IRAN—THE REAL BIG QUESTION

A few years ago we traveled to Thailand for a family vacation. There is nothing more effective than a yoga class on Koh Tau, a magical island embraced by shores of white sand and adorned with coconut trees, for creating unexpected new friendships. One afternoon, my wife returned from her yoga class and told me excitedly of a new Iranian friend whose acquaintance she had made after class. That very evening, we went out with the Iranian couple to a local club, where we sipped fruit juice and discussed life in Iran and in Israel.

The next morning I went for a morning swim to observe the colorful fish populating the various coral reefs close to the island. While standing in the warm water, putting on my mask and snorkel, I suddenly noticed my wife's Iranian friend standing in front of me.

Once we got over our initial embarrassment (natural for a meeting between an Iranian and an Israeli in bathing suits), she asked: "Aren't you afraid of swimming here, among the coral?" This innocent question deeply amused me. I smiled and said, "I'm from Israel, you're from Iran, and you are afraid to swim in the warm, tranquil waters of the coral reefs of Koh Tau?!"

As I observe the current media frenzy in Israel over the question of whether Israel intends to attack Iran's nuclear facilities, Thailand and its peaceful shores seem more distant than ever. The implicit question, one that has been with us for several years, is whether Israel can live with a nuclear Iran.

Although these are absolutely critical questions, I believe we must seek the real big question elsewhere. In the twenty-first century, anyone who has the money and the desire sooner or later will acquire nuclear weapons. Sooner or later, Iran and other hostile entities will acquire nuclear weapons. These hostile entities may not necessarily be states. Terror groups could also procure the means to launch a nuclear attack. All it takes is the desire, the money, and time.

So the real big question is not whether Israel can attack Iran, or whether Israel should attack Iran, but rather, how can Israel prepare itself to face nuclear enemies, and what must Israel do in the meantime? Yet there has been practically no public discussion of this question.

There are four reasons for the lack of debate:

One, because it is not a matter for politicians. The timeframe for politicians is usually no longer than the next few years. Naturally, their sights are always set on the next election, and in Israel elections typically take place every two to four years. So this issue will not be considered by the political leadership. The gauntlet must instead be picked up by other leaders, such as academics, rabbis, and intellectuals.

Two, this idea is very tough to absorb. The thought is so very, very unpleasant and liable to cause so very many sleepless nights...so why should Israelis think about it? After all, we have plenty of other day-to-day troubles to concern us without adding to our woes.

Three, the implications are liable to upset the most basic values of the country. A friend of mine, a successful businessman and former Israeli who moved to Palo Alto with his family, claims that Palo Alto, with its high concentration of smart, talented Jews and former Israelis, is the "Noah's Ark" of the Jewish people. As my friend sees it, Israel will eventually be doomed, so it will be up to the Jews in Palo Alto to continue the race. Spending too much time thinking about weapons of mass destruction pointed at Israel can certainly raise troubling thoughts among Israelis and might make many of them consider leaving the country.

Fourth, we have very limited means to deal with enemies who possess nuclear weapons that can reach Israel within minutes. The balance of power that has prevented the use of nuclear weapons up until now (excluding the US at the end of World War II) was maintained by a combination of mutual deterrence and of rationality on the part of the players. Let us just say that this combination is almost certainly not powerful enough to work indefinitely in our unstable neighborhood.

To sum up, the real big question is not **whether** Iran or another hostile entity will ever become a nuclear threat, but rather **how** Israel should deal with the situation **as** it happens.

July 2011

EVERY HEBREW SOLDIER MUST KNOW

"**Every Hebrew mother must know that she has put the fate of her sons in the hands of commanders who are worthy of the responsibility**"—David Ben-Gurion

This motto hangs proudly at the entrance of the IDF's Officer Training School, and the many generations of officers and commanders who passed through its doors were imbued with that spirit. They learned that they had to become commanders worthy of a great responsibility—worthy of leading the sons and daughters of Israel into battle and capable of bringing them safely back home.

The emotional sight of Gilad Shalit gaining his freedom from Hamas after five and a half years in captivity, and the process by which that freedom was gained, caused the Israeli public to see this fundamental principle in a new light and suggested another version of the motto: "Every Hebrew soldier must know that waiting at home are parents following the example of Aviva and Noam Shalit, who saved their son in his hour of need."

We were morally obligated to negotiate the release of Gilad Shalit. As soon as we knew we could not rescue him militarily, we had no choice but to reach a deal, although we knew without a shadow of doubt that the bill for the Shalit deal will come due—perhaps quite soon—and Israel will have to pay the price. We already know some of the costs: a stronger Hamas, further deterioration of our deterrence capability, increased motivation for the enemy to engage us with terror and not peace, a dangerous precedent for the future. But even knowing all this, reaching this agreement was the right thing to do.

Usually, most Israelis consider themselves security experts and political analysts, but when it came to Gilad Shalit, Israelis reacted first and foremost as parents. Israelis did not think of themselves as standing in the shoes of Binyamin Netanyahu but of standing in those of Aviva and Noam Shalit.

And that is perhaps the most significant long-term impact of the release of Shalit for us as a society and as a nation under siege in a dangerous neighborhood. This is one more sign that Israelis' faith in the state and its institutions is weakening. Israeli citizens no longer trust that their country—especially the army—will always be there for them if, G-d forbid, they or their children are ever in Shalit's situation.

Because ultimately it was not really the prime minister who gained the release of Gilad Shalit. Although he was the one who made the final decision and signed the deal, the people who created the conditions in which the prime minister had essentially no other choice were Gilad's parents. They are the real heroes of this story. With admirable modesty, dignity, determination, and self-sacrifice, Aviva and Noam mobilized the entire country. They knew they could not rely on "the system"—the army, the government—to obtain their son's freedom. Despite all the declarations and promises, "the system" has its own considerations and priorities, and Gilad's freedom was not necessarily always at the top of the list. Once the Shalits understood this, early on in the process, they took the struggle into their own hands. With the help of thousands of volunteers and supporters, they turned the release of one kidnapped soldier into the paramount national priority for the overwhelming majority of their fellow citizens. My oldest son is now in his final year of high school, after which he will enlist in the IDF. Thousands of people like me, parents of soldiers or soldiers-to-be, naturally see Aviva and Noam Shalit as role models. We whisper to ourselves, "G-d forbid I should ever be in their position, but if I am, I will follow their example."

This attitude, of reduced trust in the collective and increased trust in one's own ability to influence one's personal fate, of no longer preferring the national interest over the personal, is all of a piece with the upheavals currently sweeping the entire world. We can point to examples such as the Arab Spring that brought down tyrannical regimes and the Occupy Wall Street protests in the USA—as well as the social protests in Israel this last summer, in which the demonstrations of a few individuals metamorphosed into a wave of mass protest that changed national priorities, challenged giant corporations, threatened the influence of major power-brokers...and who knows where it will end?

Gilad Shalit is now at home, in the loving, protective arms of his family. The successful struggle of Aviva and Noam evokes awe and admiration, but it also adds one more push to the changing national priorities, perturbing the balance between the individual and society, and altering the decision-making process of the country. The change from "Every Hebrew mother must know" to "every Hebrew soldier must know" may be the most important long-term effect of the release of Gilad Shalit.

October 2011

ON PROMISES AND CAKES

How many milestones there are in bringing a Jewish child into the world and raising him and her! Many of the milestones are universal. Discovering that you are expecting. The birth. The bris. The first day of kindergarten. The first day of first grade. The bar/bat mitzvah ceremony. Graduating from high school. The wedding.

Only in Israel does the Jewish parent mark an extra significant and unique landmark—the day their child enlists into the Israel Defense Forces.

When our eldest son, Guy, was born seventeen years ago, I felt that I had a better understanding of the act of creation. His emergence from his mother's womb with a thunderous wail of self-confidence (which characterizes him to this day) confirmed my belief in a divine creator.

Like many new parents, I knew that, as small as he was, one day he would grow up. And that, I see, has happened. From the day he was born, I was already foreseeing the day he would enlist.

There is a promise in Israel that has been promised again and again, and it is the ultimate traditional promise that has never been kept. It is something akin to the promise of the arrival of the Messiah. It is the promise of fathers and mothers to their children that when they reach the age of eighteen, they will not need to carry a weapon and go to war. A few days after Guy was born, I promised my wife that our precious child would grow up in a different Israel—an Israel of peace. Those were years of great promise. Yitzhak Rabin was prime minister. The Oslo process was underway. Israeli consulates were being opened throughout the Arab world. A peace agreement was signed with Jordan. A new Middle East was peeking over the horizon. During those years, even I prepared myself for service as a soldier of peace, studying for a BA and then a master's in Middle Eastern studies, struggling night and day to learn Arabic.

And then even I, the third generation of the Melamed family living in Israel, joined those who came before me, who made a promise but didn't manage to keep it. Guy, who just celebrated his seventeenth birthday, has started the process of recruitment for army service. Tests, medical and psychological exams, and tryouts for the elite units of the IDF. And I actually thought that I and my generation would succeed where our fathers and their fathers failed.

The army experience, and the influence of the army on our lives in Israel, is felt in every corner and every place. Last week, we sat around the Seder table of the Lau-Lavi family in Hoshaya. The Lau-Lavis represent and personify the story of the resurrection of the Jewish people.

ON PROMISES AND CAKES

The grandfather of the family, Naftali, from a family of distinguished rabbis in Poland, survived the horrors of Treblinka and Buchenwald as a youth, saving his younger brother Yisrael-Meir (who went on to become the chief rabbi of Israel) as well. During his years of public service, with his wife, Joan, at his side, Naftali filled key positions in the newly established state, among them as the assistant to Moshe Dayan and as the Israeli consul in New York.

His son Shai lives in Hoshaya in the Galilee, has served in the IDF for some thirty-four years in combat and leadership positions, as well as in management and industry, and maintains an organic olive grove for his pleasure, producing excellent-quality olive oil.

Shai's sons, Moshe and Elad, naturally volunteered for the elite army units, and Moshe continues to serve as a commander in the unit in which he started out as a soldier. Shai and his wife, Varda, also have four daughters, two of whom are married, and they also have five grandchildren.

That evening the threads of our interesting conversation around the Seder table touched upon the women of the family and the heavy price exacted of the wives of career army officers. Difficult questions arose that only someone who had personally experienced this situation could understand. Is it correct for a commander who has a family to sleep at home with his wife and children during the week while his soldiers are sleeping in the field, or should he always spend the nights together with his soldiers? What is the job of senior commanders in establishing priorities and attempting to keep a balance between military responsibility and the family life of their officers? What leads a twenty-eight-year-old man to choose a military career when his wife and three children are waiting with frustration when he can't even make it home in time to carry out the mitzvah of checking the house for *hametz* (leavened food which may not be eaten during Passover) on the eve of Passover? And when does his wife declare, "Enough!"?

There were also questions that weren't asked and things that weren't said but hung heavy in the air. No one spoke of the line connecting the concentration camps of Europe from which Grandpa Naftali was saved and the army camps in Israel where his grandson Moshe is training Israel's fighters, upon whom the responsibility falls to prevent another Holocaust. Neither did anyone ask, "If we don't serve in the army then who will?"= nor even "What would happen if one day we aren't strong enough?"

The next day, we hosted a couple from Boston, who had taken advantage of the holiday to make a visit to Israel. Twenty years ago, L. and R. spent a year as volunteers at a kibbutz, and memories of that time were deeply etched in their hearts. Today, as parents of three children, in the middle of a visit as tourists in Israel, at the height of spring, when the Galilee is painted in its most glorious colors, this couple began to amuse themselves again with the idea of moving to Israel. R. asked me about the regular challenges of immigrating from the United States to Israel: making a living, where to live, language, education. For all of these questions, I could supply informed answers and advice. But then we reached the question of questions. "We are not so sure we're ready for our children to serve in the IDF," R. admitted. "That's a subject only you can decide about," I answered him. "I can tell you how much it costs to build a house in the Galilee, that, in Israel, almost everything is more expensive than in the US. That you can find good schools for the kids but not always. And that, when you immigrate to Israel, you need to be prepared to take a cut in your salary and compromise on career options. But about military service for your children, that's a discussion for you to have with your spouse."

Now back to our Guy, seventeen years old. At this point our worries are still within the framework of the theoretical and have not been put to the true, daily test. I remember how, during the four years I served in the army, my late mother, Zehava, used to say to me after Shabbat ended and I had to go back to the base, "Take care of yourself, son," and her words and the expression on her face followed me like a prayer. We still have another two or three years until the end-of-Shabbat kiss and the words that follow. In the meantime, Betsy consoles herself by saying, "What can I do? I'll do a lot of laundry and bake a lot of cakes, and God will take care of our Guy."

April 2011

ON ENTERING AND EXITING

Operation Pillar of Defense began on a Wednesday night, with Israel scoring both intelligence and operational successes. As expected, Gaza launched more rockets at the southern communities. In the background, the radio played the sad "beautiful Land of Israel" songs.

My friend Robert phoned from Beverley Hills. "It sounds like Israel is beating the war drums once again," said Robert, worried. "True," I responded, "but in Israel it's not war drums we're hearing; it's the subdued Hebrew songs that herald war or follow some other national catastrophe."

On Wednesday evening exactly one week later, I sat in the living room with my children listening to the radio reports of the ceasefire that was about to come into effect. By the time the next military operation comes around, Guy, my oldest, will probably be in uniform. "Abba, you have to write about this," urged Guy, "but try to write something optimistic."

He had not set me an easy task, writing something optimistic about a situation that does not look very optimistic. It would be easier to list some of the gains made by Hamas:

A. In addition to inundating Israel's southern communities with missiles, Hamas launched missiles over the Gush Dan region for the first time, giving the residents of central Israel a taste of what those in the south have been experiencing for a very long time—and the sky has not yet fallen. Hamas proved that Israel cannot carry out its threats. When we left Gaza, we threatened that if they carried on attacking Israel after the disengagement, they would suffer heavy consequences. They carried on attacking but suffered limited consequences. When they boasted they had the capability to reach Tel Aviv, we declared that firing missiles on Tel Aviv would be an escalation we would never accept. But the fact is we had to accept it. What next?

B. Hamas cemented its role as the leader of the Palestinian street and as the strong body with which Israel has no choice but to negotiate. The more moderate Abu Mazen has been weakened. Hamas proved once again that Israel responds only to force.

C. And perhaps the saddest of all, the levels of mutual hate, fear, and demonization have once again risen. The extremist elements on both sides have been strengthened, those who believe that there is no chance of living in peace side by side. For years, opinion has been spreading in Israel that we are destined to keep our swords for many generations more, and a large and growing portion of the Israeli public feels that is an accurate assessment of the situation.

But to survive in Israel, optimism is vital. So despite everything I listed above, what can we record as Israeli achievements in the last round of violence that (apparently) has now ended?

1. The Iron Dome system

    Jewish brains have once again proven themselves. The anti-missile defense system changed the rules of the game. Like other game-changing technology, such as the Internet or GPS, it is already difficult to remember how things were before it existed. Just thinking about life without the Iron Dome is terrifying. It may be a little early to say this, but perhaps our enemies in the south and the north will soon have to look for new ways to embitter the lives of Israelis.

2. Improved preparedness on the home front

    Government ministries, municipal authorities, the army, aid organizations, and, of course, the citizens themselves were better organized this time than during the Second Lebanon War in 2006. The process of improvement must continue because we can be sure this is not going to be the last round.

3. The IDF's sensitivity to human life and scrupulous observance of its code of ethics

    There is no other nation in the world that would take such care to avoid injuring enemy civilians during a conflict in which its own civilians are being attacked with rockets. Although there were PR considerations, these were certainly not the primary concerns. The IDF managed to hit Hamas targets while hurting the smallest possible number of innocents.

4. We seem to have achieved a period of quiet.

    We certainly could not keep on putting up with the attacks on the southern communities emanating from the Gaza Strip. In

Israel, a few years of "*relative* quiet" is still "quiet," and, as the Hebrew saying goes, "When you don't have a nightingale then even the crow is a song-bird."

5. Someone once said, "Although satisfaction is obtained by entering, wisdom lies in knowing when to exit." The Israeli leadership proved this time that it understands the limitations of force and is wise enough to withstand the pressure to "stick it to them" with a ground offensive. Understanding that it is easy to go in but much harder to leave victorious, it stopped Operation Pillar of Defense before it got bogged down in Gaza. Perhaps it was a sign that on the very day after the ceasefire, a fierce rain fell. Had there been a ground offensive instead of a ceasefire, the IDF tanks and infantry would, quite literally, have been bogged down in the heavy mud.

So we carry on living in this complex and challenging reality. A few weeks ago, my son Ari celebrated his bar mitzvah. In our family, the bar/bat mitzvah teenager donates some of their gift money to a worthy cause. Ari chose to give his donation to Yad Vashem. "Remembering the Holocaust is close to my heart," Ari explained. At the height of the conflict in Gaza, Ari asked me if I had considered building a fallout shelter for our house "just in case." "I haven't considered it," I answered, "plus a fallout shelter would be very expensive." "Maybe I could help pay for it with my bar mitzvah money," he responded. This saddened me. I would much rather my son wanted to help pay for a family trip around the world than help pay for a family fallout shelter.

For now, we need to turn our national attention to the approaching Knesset elections. The challenge: whom to vote for. This is not simple. Scanning the list of the various party leaders is not the least bit like a child in a candy store being unable to choose from the large number of tempting options. But we said we must be optimistic…

And in complete contrast to the smoke, blood, and destruction of the past week, we are just beginning to see the first leaves of cyclamens, anemones, buttercups, and other winter flowers, bringing with them the promise of the beautiful colors of an Israeli winter and of the continuity of life.

Looking forward to good news and seasonal rains,
Sagi
November 2012

HOPE

As I was leaving synagogue after Shabbat morning prayer services in Hoshaya, my friend Ido moved toward me with a teasing smile on his face. Ido is a right-winger but is open to hearing other people's opinions. From the look on his face I knew that he was looking for a debate.

"Sagi, look at this amazing country we live in," he said, waving his hand toward the Galilee hills that surround our community. "Excellent weather—we even get rain in spring! The economy is stable, the security situation is stable, unemployment is low…what else do we need in order to be satisfied?"

I thought for a moment and then replied, "You're right. But the *Titanic* also seemed fine just before it hit an iceberg and sank."

Ido cranked it up a notch. "You know, Sagi, leftists always see things backwards. During the Oslo peace process in the nineties, when buses were being blown up on the streets day and night and innocent civilians were being killed in terror attacks, the leftists claimed that we were just suffering the birth pangs of the peace process, but the future would be much brighter. Now, when security and the economy are both in good shape, but there is no peace agreement, they say the future will be catastrophic. Why can't leftists see reality as it is?"

For the rest of that Shabbat I thought about what Ido had said. Then I came to the conclusion that the problem is not actually whether we see reality for what it is. Our main problem is the **loss of hope**.

The current situation in Israel (as of mid-August 2011) certainly looks pretty good when measured against the criteria by which people usually evaluate quality of life: standard of living, employment, security, and so on. But we are gradually losing the **fundamental belief that tomorrow will be better than today.**

The hope for a better tomorrow is the essence of our national anthem, *HaTikva*—The Hope. We have not lost our hope…to be a free people in our own land. We have become a free people in our own land, and that in itself is a miracle, but along the way we have lost "the hope of two thousand years." What is that Hope? I believe it has two main components:

First, the hope for a more just society: As I write these words, the Israeli public is staging one of the most significant and widespread struggles in Israel's history. This began as a protest against the high price of cottage cheese in particular and of food in general. At the same time, public pressure is growing on Israeli legislators to limit the centralization of Israel's economy and to reduce the dominance wielded by a limited number of families in many business activities. The financial newspaper *Globes*, on the front page of its July 5 edition, said, "The social revolt will end violently… [I]n a democratic country, you cannot have 50% of the population earning just above minimum wage… the ones benefitting from this economic growth are those with capital and a very small number of senior level people." The protests have grown in recent weeks and broadened to other areas. Now we are witnessing protests that are nominally about housing prices and the working conditions of medical interns and residents but whose scope and significance are far wider-ranging and whose aftermath cannot be predicted.

I believe that the degree of centralization and the economic power of the few in Israel are not particularly bad compared with other Western countries, but there is one significant difference: Israel was not created the same way as other countries—by dividing territories between superpowers or by overthrowing monarchies. Israel was established as the fulfillment of the dream of generations, a dream for which many have paid and are continuing to pay with their blood and their lives. As citizens of a country that was established with a vision and a dream, Israelis (and many non-Israelis who are watching us with amazement) expect the world's only Jewish state to be more just, more fair, more ethical, more humane.

To a great extent, the kibbutz was the perfect example of an attempt to create a more just society. The Kibbutz Movement, which is currently celebrating its hundredth anniversary, tried to create a utopian society, to change the world, and to overcome humanity's basic instincts. Although the kibbutz has changed drastically over the last hundred years, and equality between members is now far from being the norm, it has nevertheless played a central role in building the country. Such a communal, supportive way of life, albeit in another form, could perhaps one day return to playing a central role in Israeli society.

My wife moved to Israel from the United States twenty-two years ago and joined me on my kibbutz. One evening we went to Haifa.

On the way back we went past Haifa Port, and suddenly my wife noticed a prostitute on the street. "What? There are prostitutes in Israel?!" she said, shocked. Homeless people, prostitutes, patients without proper medical care, and all the other problems of society are found everywhere in the world. But from the Jewish state, the state of the "chosen people," we all expect more.

Second, the loss of the hope for peace: The vision of a life of peace is the ultimate dream of every Israeli mother and father. The belief that although today we must fight, tomorrow our children will no longer have to do so has been the cornerstone of Israel's growth—the hope that we will not always have to "sleep with our swords." No people in the world have composed so many songs of the longing for peace. Throughout all of Israel's wars, we always saw a light in the darkness, a light that said this war was only a painful milestone along the bloody path toward peace. But in the last decade, the Israeli public has lost this hope. Maybe because we already tried it and were unsuccessful (the Oslo process), maybe because of the sense that we do not have a partner for peace (after all, we left Gaza, and in return received rockets and mortars), and maybe because we are simply physically and mentally exhausted from the quest for peace.

These two hopes—the hope for a just and ethical society and the hope for peace—are necessary for the continuity of Israel. Fulfilling the first hope depends mainly on us, the Israeli public. Fulfilling the second requires partners, but it also depends on reaching internal consensus on what peace should look like. **Returning hope to the people of Israel is the need of the hour.**

July 2011

NOT WHAT WE WERE PROMISED

Doron, kibbutz Ramat Yochanan's legendary auto mechanic, was a multi-talented and unique character. If he had not made a career out of being the best mechanic in the kibbutz movement—the kind who can fix anything that moves—he would probably have been a professor or an educator of some sort. Many kibbutz youngsters who had dropped out of the formal educational system found Doron's garage to be a safe haven and educational establishment all rolled into one, and, under Doron's guiding hand, these youngsters acquired not just mechanical skills but also values and life skills.

As a second-generation kibbutznik, the son of founders of Kibbutz Ramat Yochanan, Doron would often say, "*This isn't what we were promised.*" Apparently, on September 3, 2011, that same feeling brought nearly half a million Israelis out of their homes to protest, to declare that they expect more of their government and more **from** their government.

When the protest movement announced its "March of the Million" it was obvious to my family that we would take part. The demonstrations were held in various regions and cities the length and breadth of Israel. We debated which demonstration location we should attend. In the end, we chose the one closest to where we live, at the entrance to Moshav Kfar Yehoshua in the Yezreel Valley. On our way there we began to think that maybe the demonstration at Kfar Yehoshua had been cancelled at the last minute because the location was not mentioned at all on the radio news programs we heard; the radio ignored it completely. Apparently the broadcasters were simply ignorant of the veteran moshav, which had been established in 1927 and was named after Yehoshua Hankin, the man responsible for most of the major Zionist land purchases in the late nineteenth and early twentieth century.

During the first decades of the Zionist settlement in the Land of Israel, when someone said, "*I'm going to the valley*," everyone knew which valley they meant. The Yezreel Valley was the bastion of labor settlement, the cradle of the kibbutz movement, "THE Valley" of Israel. In daily life, by the time evening falls, the inhabitants of the valley are already cocooned in the shelter of their homes, the habits of farmers who are up before dawn to milk the cows and plow the land, people who cannot afford the luxury of a nightlife. But on this occasion the valley surprised even itself; about ten thousand demonstrators filled the cornfield, which transformed that night from a dry harvested tract of stubble into a town square filled with protesting masses.

I walked around, greeting friends and observing the diverse people at the demonstration. I saw old people and babies, farmers and philosophers, religious wearers of yarmulkes and secular wearers of tank tops. I could identify only one single common denominator: the expectation of something more for the Promised Land of Israel.

The wave of social and economic protest appears to have simply brought to the fore a feeling that had been incubating a long time but had not found a mode of popular expression prior to this summer. A feeling of "*this is not what we were promised*" and the feeling that we deserve better. A feeling that we expect more of ourselves and we expect more of our country. A feeling that the Israel of the twenty-first century is not the Israel we were promised and that we promised to ourselves and our children.

My neighbor, Yitzhak Lavi, told me a joke that seems very appropriate right now. "A kibbutznik goes into the kibbutz dining room and tells the other kibbutz members that his cat just gave birth to eight kittens: two capitalists and six socialists. The next day he goes back to the dining room and says that there are still eight kittens, but now six of them are capitalists and only two are socialists. The members ask him, 'So what changed between yesterday and today? How come all of a sudden the majority are now capitalists?' He answered, 'Today they opened their eyes.'"

Israelis feel they, too, have now opened their eyes but in a somewhat different way. The old-school socialism that had seemed to have lost its vitality has suddenly attracted Israelis who feel that, during the period when they were under the spell of capitalism and privatization, their country was stolen from them.

While attending a conference on regional economic cooperation, I sat next to a senior Israel-based American official. This period is not exactly the Golden Age of cooperation between Israel and its neighbors, and the atmosphere was a bit despondent.

Nevertheless, everyone was unanimous that even at a tense and difficult time, it is critical to keep trying. As we waited between one presentation and the next, the American official and I began talking about the social protest movement in Israel. He said he had been in Israel a year and was still trying to understand the country. I told him that even though I have lived here my whole life, I am still trying to understand it.

He shared with me some of his wisdom about the protest, using the American example. "In the States, it is considered perfectly legitimate for different members of society to reach different **outcomes**. It's fine that some people are rich and others aren't; that's the essence of the American dream. But what's not legitimate is for there to be unequal **opportunities.** In my opinion," he said, "while it's vital for Israelis to stress the importance of everyone having equal opportunities, they must also take great care not to stop people from achieving different results."

The recent wave of protest reminded Israelis of their hopes for the "Israel that we were promised" and brought them out into the town squares and the cornfields to seek their Promised Land. The soul-searching days of Rosh Hashanah and Yom Kippur are fast approaching. While we continue our quest for the land we were promised, we should remember that in fact we are already living in it—against all odds—and that its existence in our stormy neighborhood never came with a guarantee.

September 2011

WHAT CONNECTS US?

During Passover vacation I was invited to talk to Hamidrasha's *Nifgashim B'Shvil Israel,* a group that is hiking the Israel National Trail as a meaningful way to commemorate the seventy-three IDF victims of the fatal 1997 helicopter collision over moshav She'ar Yashuv. As the group's website says, it is "a unique way to meet, to have direct dialog, and to discuss basic questions about Israeli society and Jewish heritage—while hiking."

We met in the pine forest on the outskirts of Kibbutz Ramot Menashe. The three-hundred-strong group was extremely varied: men, women, and children, young adults and the elderly, religious and secular—a sampling of the entire range of ingredients in the "Israeli salad." Despite the fifteen kilometers the group had hiked that day, they were remarkably alert and attentive. I shared with them some of my musings over the past few years about Israeli society and asked for reactions from these people who were seeking common denominators for Israeli society.

In the spirit of Passover, I framed the discussion as a series of questions:

What are we really? Does the group called "citizens of the State of Israel" constitute a "compound" or a "mixture"?

Is what we are creating here, on this tiny strip of land in the heart of the Middle East, really a unique substance called "Israeli"? Or is our society perhaps only a mixture of people with shared experiences, language, rules, government institutions, threats, and history?

And from here I wondered:

What are the most meaningful common denominators that connect the citizens of Israel, and in what direction are these common denominators moving? I proposed four primary common denominators: religion, enemies, army, and culture.

Religion

I grew up in a kibbutz whose founders rejected the "religion of God"—the religion that had defined their ancestors as a people for thousands of years. Because humans are unable to live lives totally devoid of some kind of belief system, they adopted other "religions": the religion of labor and the religion of the land and nature. The famous ceremony for the *Omer* (first wheat harvest) at Kibbutz Ramat Yochanan is an example of the combination of the religion of labor with the religion of the land. At the *Omer* ceremony, held the day after the Seder night, the reapers, dressed in biblical-style finery, go out to the rustling fields of golden wheat with song and dance and harvest the first ripe grain.

The precise, rhythmic swinging of scythes in unison, the stirring dancing, the choir singing the beloved song *Shibolet BaSadeh*

("Stalks of Grain in the Field"), the smell of the field as it is reaped, the sun setting in the west, the sound of horses galloping to bring the torchbearers to light the burning banner "Raise This *Omer*" at the climax of the ceremony—all this creates a form of religious ecstasy in a pioneering community that rejected their ancestors' God of exile and created another in its place.

The *Omer* ceremony has been celebrated at Ramat Yochanan for the last sixty-seven years, but it is clear that the religion of labor and land does not have as strong roots as the religion that was rejected by its founders. Only a century has passed, a mere moment in the history of the Jewish people, yet this religion is already slowly slipping into the history books and onto the archive shelves. Followers of the religion of labor, in the kibbutz in particular and in Israeli society in general, are disappearing. The fields and orchards are gradually being converted into shopping malls and roads, the creative kibbutz ceremonies for the Shabbat and festivals are becoming a thing of the past, and kibbutz society—apart from a few islands of hold-outs who want to prove it is possible to do things differently—no longer seeks to climb barricades and smash conventions but instead has become just one more way to achieve a bourgeois life.

But even in the most extreme of those kibbutzim, God was never entirely absent. A second-generation member of my kibbutz once told me how, as a child, when he felt stressed and lonely he would secretly turn to his mother's Bible and leaf through it, reading a few verses to himself like a personal prayer. There is no prayer more genuine than that!

In contrast to the religion of labor and land, which finds itself in retreat as Israel enters its seventh decade, the religion of God is experiencing a re-awakening, although not necessarily in its traditional forms. In prayer halls in Jerusalem, in Jewish Identity Circles in the kibbutz, in newly established synagogues in Tel Aviv, in study centers across the country, the religion of God expresses itself in different ways today, but it has the same object and source of strength: a higher power, the religion of Abraham, Isaac and Jacob, Sarah, Rebecca, Rachel, and Leah—the religion of the Jews.

In 1930, the poet Bialik wrote: "One can reformulate and re-style the festivals to a certain extent, but one cannot create something from nothing... Celebrate the festivals of our ancestors and add to them something of your own...those who do not find meaning in the festivals and holy days have empty, non-spiritual souls" (*Mimekhah Eilekhah—Sefer haShabbat*, page 251).

I believe that Israel must preserve and develop the religion of Israel in order to keep together. "Israeli-ness" alone will not be strong enough glue for the long term. The religion of labor and land is in decline, a bare hundred years after its birth. It turns out that "Israeli-ness" alone cannot replace the religion of Israel.

Enemies and Cohesion

Michael, a friend from Canada, recently asked me a difficult question: "Sagi, what do you think is the biggest challenge for Israel?" I replied straight away, "The biggest challenge for us is internal cohesion. If Jews are united, nothing can defeat us. But when we are divided, our future is in great danger." Michael thought a while and then asked: "And what is the greatest threat to Israel?" I needed a few moments, and then I said, "The biggest threat hanging over us is if in the future our enemies become united." "What's the difference between those two things—the challenge and the threat?" said Michael. "The challenge depends mostly on us," I answered, "and the threat depends mostly on others."

There are those who say, "When we have peace and are no longer surrounded by enemies, we will begin to fight among ourselves. Israel's enemies need only wait quietly and let the Jews destroy each other. " These words express the concern—a concern that is not totally unfounded—that one day our enemies will stop attacking us and will let us internalize all our fears, bitterness, and jealousies and then harm each other. Our most significant social glue is living together on a tiny island in an unstable neighborhood, surrounded by those who wish us ill. But is having enemies in common sufficient to keep Israeli society together? And is this a healthy way to do it?

The Army As a Molding and Unifying Experience

A few weeks ago, my family went for our periodic eye exams at our HMO clinic in Tiberias. Doctors are paid by the number of patients they see, so their time is short—approximately seven minutes per patient. The amount of time and attention the doctor is able to devote is extremely limited, but on this visit our children received exemplary attention.

I was the first one in. "I know you!" I said when I saw the eye doctor. At first he was reluctant to waste precious moments of his limited time with polite greetings. But then we began the well-known Israeli ritual: "Where did you serve in the army, what division?" We discovered that about twenty-five years ago I was his instructor in a tank commander's course… after that, it was a short distance to the personal attention for my children and the battle stories from our shared time serving in the military service.

Even before Israel was established, the paramilitary groups that pre-dated the IDF (Palmach, Haganah, Lechi, and others) were Israel's melting pot. You went in as a kibbutznik/moshavnik/new immigrant/city dweller/whatever, and came out an Israeli and an army veteran. This does not mean that army service, in which one learns to kill or be killed, is necessarily the best way to unite people from different backgrounds, but that is a topic for another discussion.

The melting pot that is the army is being eroded. Our model of army service is now marching toward the American model, an army in which most of the soldiers are those who want a stable income and a path to social mobility.

The Israel Defense Forces is becoming less and less "the army of the people" in which everyone serves and more an army that defends the people but in which only some serve. While there will always be Israelis who serve for ideological reasons, wanting to serve their country in a meaningful way, the fear is that the IDF may become predominantly an army of the poorer and less educated, those who feel they have few other ways to advance in society.

If so, what is the alternative to army service as a common denominator and unifier? Can Israel dispense with the social role the army has played in unifying the country since the establishment of the state? Is it possible to create a framework for civilian national service in which every citizen in the country will participate and, during their service, will be exposed to and mix with each other?

Culture and Way of Life

It is difficult to find an accurate definition for "authentic Israeli culture." The culture that has developed in Israel is a fascinating synthesis of religious heritage, national revival, and facets of many other cultures, plus a smidgen of battle dust, a pinch of landscape, all spiced with nature and wrapped up in the world's oldest living language.

Government authority was also a central part of Israeli culture. There are many examples, among them the rejection, during Israel's first thirty years, of the culture of immigrants from North Africa and, on the other hand, the one-time ban on playing on official media channels songs that were considered liable to reduce national motivation (the most infamous example being *Shir laShalom,* "Song for Peace").

But in recent years it seems that commercial considerations are more and more determining the direction of Israeli culture—not ideology but profit. How else can one explain the Israeli public's addiction to reality programs that show a group of attention-seekers who voluntarily allow themselves to be filmed shut up in a house for three months, with commercials being inserted in between one scene and the next?

During Passover I watched the movie *The Hunger Games* with my older children. It was too violent for my taste, but my teenagers insisted on watching it. *The Hunger Games* presents a dystopia centered on an extreme reality program. According to the movie, if today most reality shows harm only our intelligence and waste our time, tomorrow they may have the potential to damage our freedom and our lives.

"Start-Up Nation" or "Built to Last"?

Many years ago, Martin Buber wrote of the kibbutz movement that "the kibbutz is an idea that has not yet failed." This cautious approach is also appropriate for the questions before us. We are living in a country that is still a work in progress.

If we can draw comparisons with the business world, we seem to be in the "start-up" phase. *Start-Up Nation*, the best-selling book by Dan Senor and Saul Singer, looks at the entrepreneurial talents of Israelis who have turned their country into a hothouse of start-ups. Singer and Senor focus more on the successes and less on the difficulties of start-ups, of which there are many. Jim Collins, in his book of business management *Built to Last*, explores the secrets of success not of start-ups but of established companies that were built on strong and healthy foundations. One of Israel's difficulties is the challenge of strengthening the qualities that are required to turn Israeli society from "start-up" to "built to last."

So what really connects us, and what is our common denominator, we citizens of the State of Israel? Is Israeli society a compound or a mixture? And when—if ever—will we have completed our "start-up" phase?

April 2012

FEARS

"Yesterday, I went to a ceremony honoring the memory of Irwin Green, a very special man from Detroit who worked tirelessly toward bringing Jews and Arabs closer together," I told my daughter Sivan over breakfast, before she headed off for another day in first grade. "Where?" she asked. "In Nazareth," I replied. "In Upper Nazareth, where the kindergarten teachers live?" she continued. "Not in Upper Nazareth—in Arab Nazareth," I answered. "What? Arabs live there? Arabs like the Greeks? Arabs are cruel, right, Dad?" Sivan had evidently drawn an association with the Hannukah story she'd heard in class just a few days earlier.

When I returned that same night from the ceremony for Mr. Green, I asked my older son, Guy, who is seventeen years old, how many of his classmates ever spoke with an Arab youth their age. Guy is unusual among his friends in his exposure to those outside his immediate community. Not only because of his father. He volunteers in the Magen David Adom (Israeli Red Cross) along with

Arab youth and played volleyball with a team in the Arab village of Ilabun. An Arab team, one of the tops in the league. "Dad, I'm no example, but, other than me, most of the kids my age never exchanged a word with an Arab, unless you count the Bedouin security guard at the school or the Arab cook who works in the catering on Shabbat."

A few months ago, little Sivan went for a walk with a friend in our community of Hoshaya on a Shabbat afternoon, and the two of them disappeared. After two hours of frantic searching, in the intense heat of the Israeli summer, we found them next to the grocery store, hunting for treasures. As we returned home, my beloved daughter's hand safely in mine, we saw the Arab security guard who patrols the community on Shabbat. "You see, Sivan? Even Hoshaya's guard was out looking for you," I said, trying to impress her. "But, Dad," she replied, "are guards allowed to drive on Shabbat?" "He's not Jewish," I explained. "He's Arab, and that's why he can drive on Shabbat." "But, Dad, aren't Arab people bad? Isn't he dangerous for us?" The realization that the guard who protects us is actually Arab, I could see, was terrifying.

Recently a survey was published by the Israeli Institute for Democracy. Its worrisome results showed that, among Israel's Jewish population, there has been an increase in the suspicion, distrust, and fear of Arab citizens.

Fear is perhaps the main factor that feeds the flames of the Israeli-Arab conflict and what prevents any movement forward toward reaching a solution. In parallel, fear is the factor in this conflict for which a solution (to fear) is not a zero-sum solution. In other words, the allocation of lands between the two sides of the conflict is more problematic since every bit of land that goes to one side is taken from the other. On the other hand, fear is an emotion that, if reduced on one side, does not take anything away from the other.

Why are we and our children afraid of our Arab neighbors? What is the source of this fear? I tried to put together an inventory list of fear factors:

Education and Myth: We have been raised from our earliest days on a very simple approach: we are good, and they are bad. Darkness helps emphasize the light, and white stands out against black. If you want it to be clear who are the **good** guys then you need to emphasize who are the **bad** ones.

The series of books I loved as a child was *The Young Athletes.* On those pages, Alon the Forward and Rafi the Goalie brought victory and honor to the young State of Israel—something that the Israeli national soccer team was never able to do. These stories inevitably featured a villain, sometimes Nazi but usually Arab, who tried through his devious ways to confound the young heroes on their way to fame and glory. A similar theme was also found in other popular books such as the *Hasamba* series, *Azit the Paratrooper Dog*, and others. Physical fitness, willpower, determination, rigorous training—and even romance—were not enough to ignite the spirit of the young reader. There had to be an evil Arab to spice up the story, and if he had a big and dirty mustache and black eyes piercing with fury, so much the better.

Even in Israel's holidays, the theme of the good versus the bad sets the tone. Except for the New Year holidays and Tu b'Shvat, where the seasons of the year and nature play a major role, in all the other holidays—Hannukah, Purim, and Pesach—there are the "bad guys" (Egyptians, Greeks, Romans, Persians, Amalekites), who are vanquished by the "good guys" (us). A wise Jew once explained to me that all Israeli holidays come down to one thing: "They wanted to kill us. We killed them. Let's eat!"

An easier way to explain things to children and also to ourselves: imagine the Hannukah story as follows. The Greek Empire had spread throughout the world and was influencing the countries it conquered in many ways, both positive and negative. On the one hand, they espoused materialism, worship of the strong and the beautiful, and dismissal of the spiritual and abstract. On the other hand, they brought with them advanced technologies, better medical care, and municipal order. Even among the Jews within the kingdom of Judah there were different streams. One embraced progress, science, and coexistence with the surrounding peoples, including making compromises on principles for the sake of peace in the kingdom. Another stream was nationalistic, strictly adherent to tradition and to obeying the rules of the sacred teachings as they understood them. This latter group was ready to sacrifice life and livelihood in the name of following religious principles. Sound familiar? Perhaps. Sound simple and easy to explain? I'm not so sure.

Language: Encounters with a foreign language can cause fear and alienation. The Arabic vocabulary of the average Israeli Jew is limited to a few words of slang that have penetrated into Hebrew, such as "*Kif,*" "*Sakhten,*" and "*Ahalan,*" as well as some useful key phrases from the army, such as, "Halt or I'll shoot you." Even important initiatives for teaching Arabic in schools frequently fail because of the children's deep-seated fear of a language they perceive as belonging to the enemy. A deeper understanding of the Arabic language would enable Jewish Israelis not only to better appreciate its richness and multitude of expressions but would mainly remedy a situation whereby every call of the Muslim *Muazzin* to prayer sounds to the Jewish ear like a call to arms.

Political Considerations: Unfortunately, the power of fear as a means to enlist citizens for political support is usually stronger than the power of hope. For this reason, many politicians cynically but effectively inspire fear in their constituents as a way to engage them and secure their support. The further Israel moves away from a longed-for peace and the deeper the belief that there is no one to talk to penetrates further into the national consciousness, along with the conviction that the whole world is against us, the power and centrality of fear increases as an effective means for political manipulation.

Trauma of Persecution: "That fact that you're paranoid doesn't mean they aren't out to get you," goes a wise saying. The Jewish people are indeed steeped in persecution, terror attacks, and attempts of extermination. In the historical perspective, we are still in the same period when the Holocaust of the Jewish people took place. Thus, in spite of everything written above, the Jews have a good and proven reason to believe, as it is written in the Pesach Haggadah, that "in every generation someone is attempting to exterminate us." Among those who have persecuted and attacked Jews over the last hundred years, Arabs have a place of honor. Without any need for deep investigations, clearly Israeli paranoia is based in reality!

The Arab population also has a part in the balance of fear. Why are the Arabs afraid of the Jews?

History: The State of Israel was established in the heart of the Middle East, surrounded by Arab nations and peoples. Even those who don't believe in the Divine intervention can't remain indifferent to the remarkable way a state was created for and by Jews who barely survived systematic extermination of their people in Europe. Yet in the process, and during the military conflicts that arose every few years afterward, the victims were the Arab residents of the land. Even if you take into account the progress and relative economic wellbeing that came along with the blossoming of Zionism in Israel, the local Arabs became the conquered, refugees, and second- or even third-class citizens. This is a historical fact.

The minority is generally suspicious of the majority: the Jewish majority has the strength in Israel. Even in countries that are calmer and less conflicted than Israel, the minorities often suspect and fear the majority—although certainly not as much as when the peoples of the minority and the majority are still in the midst of a blood-soaked, existential conflict.

Incitement: As many Jewish politicians make cynical use of fear of Arabs to reinforce a general feeling of anxiety, so do their Arab counterparts. When an Arab politician is supported by a nationalist and belligerent platform, and when those who call for following a path of peace are perceived in the Arab public as defeatists, it's no wonder that the voice of fear is heard louder and more clearly.

So what do we do with all this?

A simple, easy solution does not exist in our neighborhood. I usually find myself telling visitors and friends from overseas that it is impossible, and even forbidden, to look at the Israeli situation and the spectrum of problems and challenges it faces through black/white or right/wrong glasses. "Whoever tries to tell you that the solutions are simple is either blind, a liar, or both," I explain to them. Still, recognizing fear as being at the root of the Arab-Jewish conflict is critical. This would enable us to separate between fears and the real, significant, and complex issues such as demography, geography, and division of resources, on the one hand, and focus on ways to deal with our mutual fears, such as getting to know "the other," learning their language, creating dialogue, and breaking down stereotypes, on the other.

December 2010

FROM A DISTANCE EVERYTHING IS NEARER

It is late afternoon, and I'm on my way to a meeting in Kfar Vradim, a lively Jewish settlement next to the Tefen industrial area in the Western Galilee. Kfar Vradim was established in the 1980s by Stef Wertheimer, the legendary industrialist, and a group of partners, as a new model for quality settlement in the country's northern periphery.

The route to Kfar Vradim took me through the city of Carmiel. Topping the crest of the hill that stretches from west to east over Carmiel, I stopped to take in the expansive view. The landscape in front of me was breathtaking for two reasons: first, because the Galilee at this point in the late winter/early spring is sparkling green, highlighted by bright patches of color. Even the usual eyesores—the quarries and ad hoc garbage dumps—are obscured by a veil of green and flowers. These are the days when the Galilee is at its most glorious, like a bride under the huppa, when her scars and discolorations are hidden under a heavy layer of makeup and the happiness of the wedding day. And, secondly, each time I see this view, I am impressed (on the one hand) and worried (on the other) by the mosaic of settlements and communities in the Galilee. Carmiel is situated right in the center of the Galilee, and around it are scattered a number of small Jewish settlements, kibbutzim, moshavim, and communal villages, which are generally perched on the tops of hills, in defiance and for protection. Around them are large Arab villages, generally built, according to the finest tradition, at the base and slopes of the hills to take full advantage of the fertile valley lands.

While I was standing there, breathing in the clear air and enjoying the view, a white car stopped next to me, and a young man got out. He looked Arab but was dressed like an American. He walked over to a large rock and looked out over the peak, in the direction of the Muslim village of Dir el Assad. Totally focused on the landscape below, he took out a camera and started to take pictures. I went over to him and started a conversation. The words flowed out of him easily, without hesitation, as if he was just waiting to be asked to share his feelings. His name is Mustafa, he told me, and he was born in Dir el Assad, the town he was taking a picture of. He has a wife and son. He is Muslim. For the last ten years he has been living in the US, in Orlando, Florida. He left Israel because he wanted a change of scene and to try to make his way in a new place. He'd only been back to visit once during those ten years. He works in a cell phone store in Orlando. He deeply misses the Galilee and his village, the family values, and the community life, but in the US he has a chance to advance, to earn more. I asked him what he misses most. "Everything," he answered. "But most of all this view of my village. There is no view like this in America. I love this land. The first thing I did when I arrived was to come up here to look at the village from above and capture this view in a picture."

I asked Mustafa what he thought about Jewish-Arab relations. He explained that many Jews live in Orlando, as well as many Arabs, and they live and work very nicely one next to the other. "Only here in Israel there's a 'balagan' (mess). If you want to see how Arabs and Jews can live together, only in the United States. There, everyone respects everyone as equals. Just here there's 'balagan,'" he repeated.

I asked permission to take his picture, and I continued on my way to Kfar Vradim, on a road that winds between olive groves and stone terraces. As I drove, I wondered to myself why in Orlando Jews and Arabs live so nicely together, and here in Israel there is 'balagan' between them. Could it be the distance from the centers of tension? Perhaps the foreign language? Or perhaps it is the shared background and similar cultures of the Middle Easterners that connect them and create a common ground, ironically in a foreign land? What enables Mustafa and his Israeli-Jewish friends in Orlando to develop relationships that they can't manage to do as neighbors in Israel?

Still buried in my thoughts, I arrived at Kfar Vradim, with its beautifully landscaped grounds and homes for some fifteen hundred families. In the center of the town there is a well- equipped country club, a commercial center, school, and everything a community needs to live comfortably in a lovely, rustic Galilee landscape. With a little time remaining until my meeting, I decided to look around the town and get a taste of the atmosphere. As a sports enthusiast, I naturally gravitated to the country club. Following my senses of smell and hearing, I found my way to the room where a martial arts class was underway. It looked like a mixture of karate, ju jitsu, and tae kwan do. But it wasn't the technique that caught my attention but the mixture of people and languages in the class. The two instructors were young, powerful, Arabic-speaking men (Druze, Muslim, or Christian—it's hard to tell). And practicing with them were about fifteen kids between the ages of seven and twelve. Most of them were Arab, and some were Jewish. But it was the language of instruction that amazed me. The teachers spoke in a mixture of three languages! Arabic (their mother tongue and that of some of the students), Hebrew (mother tongue of some of the students and the national language of Israel), and English, which seemed to be the official language of this type of integrated martial arts. Thus, when the teacher ordered a child to kick at three different heights, each height got its own language: *"ras"* (head in Arabic), "middle," and *"regel"* (leg in Hebrew).

In the month of Adar, a time when it is a mitzvah to be happy, on the eve of Purim, a week after the shocking murder of the Fogel family in Itamar, as the cars of Arab students are torched at Safed College and the level of tension and racism in Israel steadily rises, Mustafa from Dir el Assad and his Jewish friends in Orlando, and the participants in the martial arts course in Kfar Vradim, show that, in spite of everything, it is possible.

March 2011

SABRAS

Most Israelis would be happy to swap August for any other month of the year. In August, parents are driving themselves crazy trying to keep their children busy and entertained. Children who were perfectly happy to amuse themselves in July, relaxing after the school year and enjoying summer activities, are now complaining, "I'm bored!" and spending most of their time teasing their siblings, watching movies, and playing on the computer. Employers in all sectors of the economy call this the "slow season" because workers are on vacation, off taking care of their children, or are simply infected by the end of the summer.

Israelis who take their vacations in Israel face many challenges. In August in a tiny, crowded country there is almost no place of refuge from the hordes of people who are also searching unsuccessfully for a quiet corner in which to relax. Furthermore, vacationers have to pay prices that are much higher than what they would pay for equivalent styles of vacations in other places in the world. In August it is difficult not to be jealous of people who live in larger countries with open borders, who can go on vacation for a reasonable cost and *without* having to use an airport.

The weather in August is another challenge. Heat waves are frequent, and the cool breezes that herald the arrival of autumn are still not expected for another month or two. And the biggest reminder of the long summer is the colors of the landscape. Israel in August is dusty brown and yellow, with perhaps here and there a touch of light green. It is as if an imaginary artist, while painting Israel's summer landscape, had run out of paints except for a few faded and dry colors. Israel in August is a dry, dusty place in desperate need of refreshment and renewal.

One weekday morning in early August I set out for a brisk walk between Hoshaya and Moshav Tzipori. Moshav Tzipori borders with Tzipori National Park, where, almost two thousand years ago, Rabbi Yehuda HaNasi wrote the Mishnah. I set out early, before sunrise and before the air became hot and humid. The morning was still fresh as the birds chirped a greeting to the new day.

When I had climbed up from the small valley that separates Hoshaya and Tzipori and was approaching the gate of the moshav, I noticed two men. They were standing about fifty yards apart with their backs to me, each one holding a long stick at the end of which was a small tin can. Their attention was focused on picking sabra fruits from the green hedge of sabra plants, standing like a natural wall on both sides of the narrow road that leads from Hoshaya to Tzipori. Skillfully pushing the little tin can beneath the yellow-red fruit, they twisted the sabra off the cactus with one half turn and then deposited the fruit into a large collection bucket. Early morning is the best time to pick sabras. It is still cool, and there is no wind to blow the tiny little thorns off the sabra plants and into exposed parts of the body.

The sabra is not exactly the most popular fruit in Israel. It is difficult to pick, it scatters small thorns in every direction, and, because of its hard seeds, it causes constipation. Nevertheless, native-born Israelis are referred to as "Sabras" because they are prickly and rough on the outside but soft and sweet inside.

Watching the two men pick sabras in August reminded me of my childhood. In summer we would hike from the kibbutz to the abandoned Arab village of Hosha near the town of Shfar'am, large plastic buckets in our hands, to pick the figs, pomegranates, and sabras that grew among the houses that were abandoned by their inhabitants after they fled in 1948.

I wondered who owned those sabras between Hoshaya and Tzipori and whether the two men were supposed to be picking them. I went up to the older man and asked him, "Whose sabras are those?" He turned to me with a mix of defiance and apprehension. "This is public land; they don't belong to anyone," he said before returning to his work with great concentration. I decided to try my luck with his younger companion.

I approached him and wished him good morning then asked, "Whose sabras are these?" His answer was similar. "No one's. The land's." I asked permission to photograph him, and he refused. I asked again, promising to photograph him from behind so his face would not be seen but only the picking would be documented. This time he agreed. I photographed him and returned home. The sun had already begun to rise in the east and was getting in my eyes.

As I walked briskly, I remembered the story our friend R. from Moshav Tzipori once told us. R. and her husband built their house there about twenty-five years ago, when the moshav was still struggling and before the booming housing market in the north of Israel turned it into an upscale community. R.'s family is like a walking advertisement for the Jewish Agency. The parents, both of whom are graduates of prestigious American universities, made aliya (immigrated to Israel) and settled in the Galilee. Their children (three sons and one daughter) are all officers in the IDF, and two of them are combat pilots.

On the land that the couple purchased are rows of sabra cactuses. One day, R. and her husband noticed several Arab men on their property picking the sabras. When they asked them why they were trespassing, the Arab pickers told them, "This is our land. We are from Safouriya. The sabras have belonged to our family forever." As they continued to talk, R. and her husband learned that they were the descendants of residents of the Arab village of Safouriya, a large Arab community that at one point in its long history had been the largest Arab settlement in the Galilee.

The inhabitants of Safouriya had abandoned their village in the summer of 1948, during the War of Independence. In 1949, Moshav Tzipori was established in its place, on the ruins of the village of Safouriya and next to Tzipori, the ancient Jewish settlement of the Mishnaic period. Many former inhabitants of the abandoned village of Safouriya have lived since that time in Nazareth, near Moshav Tzipori, and they still consider it to be their land, albeit temporarily under Jewish occupation.

Since they consider the lands and the fruit orchards of Moshav Tzipori to belong to them, they see nothing wrong with picking the sabras there. In fact, R. told me that she had told them that they could pick the fruit but should just let her know ahead of time when they were coming. "There's enough for all of us," she told them. They refused point-blank. "This is our land, we inherited it, and we will absolutely not let you know ahead of time."

I recently went with my family to see the protest tents on Rothschild Boulevard in Tel Aviv. I had to see with my own eyes the protests for social justice and try to understand it. I still do not understand it completely, nor do many other people. As we walked in the sweaty Tel Aviv air among the tents planted along the boulevard, I suddenly heard the voice of veteran singer Si Hyman coming from one of the tents. One of her famous songs is "Big Hero," and the words are as relevant today as when they were first written: *"Wars no longer happen in summer, even for us it's too hot for hatred."*

In August 2011, between one heat wave and the next, between a demonstration and a protest tent, between inhabitants of yesterday and inhabitants of today, between the conflict that was and the conflict that is sure to come, we see that the Israeli experience swings between the two extremes of the sabra—from prickly and hard to soft and sweet.

August 2011

EACH SIDE MANAGES TO CONVINCE ME THAT THE OTHER SIDE IS RIGHT

"Each side manages to convince me that the other side is right. When I talk to Israeli rightists, I feel like a total leftist. When I listen to Muslim religious leaders, I'm sure the rightists are right," said a frustrated Rabbi David Bigman during a recent phone conversation.

Rabbi Bigman put into words the agonizing frustration of many in the "moderate peace camp" in Israel. The current situation is far too complex to present as black and white, good and bad.

I think life must be much more straightforward for people on one or other of the extremes.

If you are dedicated to the eternal unity of the biblical Land of Israel, to Jewish control of holy sites such as the Cave of the Patriarchs, and to Jewish settlement throughout the Promised Land; if, for you, the war over the Land of Israel is eternal, and the People of Israel are fated to live by the sword forever, the people around us are malevolent and are waiting for the right moment to destroy us, and the present struggle is simply one of many in a long, drawn-out war going back to the days of the Patriarch Abraham; if you believe that giving our enemies an inch will just cause them to demand a mile—then obviously we cannot give up one single iota of land. We must set down roots within the lines that were established when we won a just war in 1967 and not yield to the intense international pressure to withdraw. We must weaken our potential enemies as much as possible and not let them develop national institutions, symbols of sovereignty, or armed forces.

On the other hand, if you are convinced that ruling over another people gradually eats away at the soul of Israel like a cancer, eroding our morality and our standing in the community of nations; if you believe we cannot maintain long-term control over another people; if you hear the warning bells of danger if Israel continues in its current direction; if, for you, concepts such as "Palestinian State" that once were whispered in secret and considered evidence of a lack of patriotism are today the need of the hour; if you believe that six million Jews in Israel cannot live forever in a state of armed readiness, surrounded by hundreds of millions of enemies while slowly losing the Jewish majority between the Jordan River and the Mediterranean Sea—then obviously we must withdraw from the occupied territories and stop governing another people, as soon as we can find someone willing to take them off our hands.

In December 1987, I was a tank platoon commander in the vicinity of Ramallah, where we were supposed to spend a week in ongoing security activities. But we ended up staying there for three months as part of the First Intifada. During this challenging period I was exposed to the injustices of Israel's occupation. Ever since

EACH SIDE MANAGES TO CONVINCE ME THAT THE OTHER SIDE IS RIGHT

then I have been convinced that our rule over millions of Palestinians is not moral, cannot continue long term, and damages the character, image, and future of the Jewish population of Israel.

Those who point out that the occupied territories were acquired in a justified defensive war are correct. It is also indisputable that many other countries around the world, including those we consider advanced and enlightened, have occupied and oppressed other people, and yet no one demanded that they give back land. But we were born Jews, for better or for worse. The occupation is bad, and it is damaging us.

So if the occupation is bad for both us and the Palestinians then the solution would seem to be simple. Give it back. Withdraw. Two states for two people.

There might very well be a majority in Israel who would support such a solution, difficult and painful though it would be. But here we come to a major stumbling block. As the saying goes, "Just because you're paranoid it doesn't mean they're **not** after you." I am not at all convinced that the other side intends to live next to us in peace or is willing to let go of its grandiose dreams of kicking out all the Jews (if not throwing them into the sea). I fear a situation in which we will be dependent on the good will, morality, and justice of them and not of ourselves.

There are many reasons for this fear. Here are three major ones:

One: The Palestinian leadership that is currently seeking recognition in the UN institutions does not represent all the Palestinian people. Hamas, which controls Gaza, is unequivocal in its opposition to the two-state solution and calls openly and consistently for Israel's destruction. Signing a peace agreement with the PA today would be like shaking hands with an enemy that is trying to stab you with the other hand.

Two: The Palestinians do not recognize Israel's right to be a Jewish country. If they do not consider Israel to have the right to exist as a Jewish country, even within a smaller footprint (the pre-1967 lines with adjustments), then where on earth does Israel have that right?

Three: Arab citizens of Israel, who constitute about 18 percent of the country's citizenry, are beginning to identify themselves more and more with their Palestinian brethren and to define themselves as "part of the Palestinian people and the Arab nation" (from the foreword to "Future Vision for Palestinian Arabs in Israel," a document that was written in 2006 by the National Committee of Heads of Arab Local Authorities in Israel). The fear that the next stage of Palestinian demands for land and independence will concentrate on the Galilee, which has been part of Israel since the founding of the country, is not entirely unfounded.

So the challenge is to convince the centrists in Israel of the trustworthiness of our Palestinian neighbors. The Israeli public requires unambiguous proofs from the Palestinians—not a one-time statement but many concrete deeds over the course of time—that demonstrate they truly are preparing themselves to live in peace with Israel. Israeli peace activists make comments such as, "They can't say something like that out loud because they fear the extremists in their midst" or "The frustration and rage of forty-four years of occupation is too great, and so it's too hard for them." Maybe those things are true. But that is not enough to convince those of us who believe that the occupation must end yet at the same time fear for the fate of the Jewish State of Israel.

EACH SIDE MANAGES TO CONVINCE ME THAT THE OTHER SIDE IS RIGHT

The Israeli peace camp and its Palestinian friends have, up until now, invested most of their efforts in convincing the Israeli side of the conflict that we must reach a two-state solution. The time has come to invest more effort in the Palestinian side. If the Palestinians are really serious about living alongside us in peace, they must rise to the challenge and invest in a thorough, comprehensive program of convincing actions. Convincing us. The Palestinian people must prove to their Jewish neighbors that the establishment of an independent Palestinian state alongside Israel is not an act of national suicide on Israel's part.

October 2011

STREET CAT

"On Saturday afternoon I rode my bike along the Herzliya beach, with my dog running beside me," said Danny Hakim. "When we got to the Sidnah Ali Mosque, my dog was suddenly surrounded by a pack of street cats. He went for the smallest cat and bit it on the chest. I quickly got off my bike to see if I could help the luckless creature. While I was busy examining the cat and slowly realizing that its minutes were numbered, the custodian of the mosque suddenly appeared next to me. It turns out he had witnessed the entire unfortunate incident from the roof of the mosque.

"'It's your fault!' he cried. 'You must pay!' His wife followed him out, screaming and yelling, 'The poor cat! Our poor cat!' I was amazed at the excessive sense of sentiment toward what had, after all, until a few moments earlier been simply an abandoned street cat, one of many."

Danny Hakim took a deep breath, smiled apologetically, and continued his story. "I told the angry couple that I was sorry, and I apologized. I asked them what they wanted me to do. The mosque custodian declared that first we must bury the cat. We took spades and buried him, digging energetically side by side. It was a bizarre sight: a Jew and a Muslim burying a street cat one afternoon on the beach of Herzliya. When we had finished burying the cat, I asked him what else he would like me to do. 'You must now pay for the cat that your dog murdered!'

"I explained that it was Shabbat," continued Danny, "and on Shabbat I don't carry money. I told him that I would return the next day and bring him the money." The custodian refused. "If you can't pay immediately then leave your dog with us as a guarantee that you will return with the money!" Danny refused to leave his dog and repeated his promise to return. "I deliberately kept my bike helmet on, in case of trouble." I should mention that Danny Hakim is a karate master (a sixth Dan black belt, world-championship silver medalist) and is also someone who works to promote peace. He is the founder and chair of Budo For Peace, *http://www.budoforpeace.org*, an organization that creates bridges between Jewish and Arab youth via martial arts training.

My friend Danny Hakim told the story of the street cat during an evening of job interviews for a new manager of Budu For Peace. When he reached this point in the story, he tossed the conversational ball to the interviewee and asked him, "What would you have done at that point?" The interviewee kept his composure, thought for a moment then answered, "I would have gone the next day to a pet store to ask how much a top-quality cat would cost, photograph the price with my mobile phone, and go back to the mosque and pay the custodian double the price of the cat in the store."

Everyone in the room turned to Danny. "So what did you do in the end?" Danny said he still hadn't done anything. He intended to get advice from a few more friends and then decide.

A week later Danny told me how the story continued. "I asked for advice from three Arab karate trainers that I know. I asked a Jordanian trainer and two Israeli Arab trainers: one a Bedouin man and the other a devoutly religious Muslim woman. The Israelis didn't think it was a big deal and advised me to pay the custodian a small sum and then forget about it. The Jordanian advised me to buy a new cat for him.

"When I came home from my short trip to Jordan, I went back to the mosque with an envelope containing a fifty-shekel note in my pocket. I wanted to see how the custodian would react when he opened the envelope and saw the amount of compensation. At the steps of the mosque I was spotted by a giant of a man who resembled a sumo wrestler. He asked me what I wanted. I asked to see the custodian. He called out to the custodian in a thin soprano voice that was in surprising contrast with his huge size, and his call disturbed the scores of cats that ran around the mosque.

"The custodian appeared, and he recognized me immediately. He invited me in and asked me to join him on the patio, while introducing me to the mother of the dead cat. His wife came into the room, looking as if she was still mourning her loss. He sent her to bring refreshments. It was a bright day, and the air was clear and cool on the beach of Herzliya. We both sat and drank bitter coffee from small cups, enjoying the view and the weather. My host slowly opened up and told me about his life and his family. He has lived at the mosque for twenty-five years and has eight children and thirteen grandchildren.

"Now I broached my reason for coming. Despite the mild weather and the pleasant atmosphere in the room, I preferred to complete my business before the sumo wrestler returned. I told the custodian about the advice I had received from my friends. I said that as a goodwill gesture I had brought with me a compensation payment for the dead cat, and I handed over the envelope with the cash.

"The custodian opened the envelope, looked at the money, and said that he didn't expect a monetary payment because no amount of money could bring the cat back to life…and in the same breath he asked me if I wanted to donate the money to the mosque. I told him it was his decision. We sat for a while and drank more coffee, a kind of meditation in honor of our new friendship, discussed our joint hopes for life in Israel, and then parted as friends."

Danny ended his story of the street cat with a deep breath. "Danny," I said, "what lessons do you take from this story? How does it relate to the reality of our life here?"

"Oho…" responded Danny with his Australian-Japanese accent. "There are several lessons! But the central lesson is the one of taking a conflict and turning it into an opportunity. He is a devout Muslim, and I am a believing Jew. He lives in a mosque on the beach of Herzliya, and I live in Herzliya Pituah. The conditions for conflict are ripe and present in the differences of background, language, and religion, even before the sad incident with the cat.

"I could have ignored the conflict between us after the bloody meeting between my dog and his street cat. I didn't have to go back to the mosque. I could have forgotten the entire thing and never seen him again. That's what most of my Arab friends advised me to do. But despite that I chose to turn the negative meeting into an opportunity to create something positive, to break down stereotypes, to build trust and mutual respect. I chose to confront the conflict face to face, to try to replace it with understanding and harmony.

"I also had to deal with my own fear," acknowledged Danny. "I had butterflies in my stomach when I went back to the mosque with the money in my pocket. I didn't know what kind of reception I would receive. It would have been easier to listen to the fear that told me to keep away from that threatening, angry place, not to return to the scene of the incident. But instead of giving in to the fear I chose to overcome it.

"And so," concluded Danny Hakim, "after we sat and finished our coffee together, the custodian and I, in his home, and I had apologized and accepted responsibility for the incident and shown willingness to pay compensation, we showed each other basic respect and also opened up our hearts to each other a little and got to know each other personally as human beings…that was when the dead cat become part of the past and instead our joint future became the central topic."

Any possible connection between Danny Hakim's story and the various religious, national, and sectarian conflicts in our stormy neighborhood and the possible courses of action available to us will be the sole responsibility of the reader to determine.

February 2012

PEACE DUTY

Reserve duty, an army base somewhere in the south. After midnight. War games. Two-way radios and telephones crackling. "Dragon, this is Tiger, over." Forces mobilizing. Missions assigned. Destroying targets. Maneuver and fire.

A clutch of reserve soldiers, bleary-eyed and whisker-stubbled, are manning the control posts. Twenty-year-olds to men in their sixties, in faded army fatigues, they come from every conceivable background—lawyers, government bureaucrats, farmers, hi-tech'ers. Entering reserve duty, each one dons his uniform, assumes his army position, and is magically transformed into an intelligence officer, operations sergeant, medical officer, or tank battalion commander. They've all left their comfortable "civilian world" behind to focus on the military agenda at hand.

Between the changing of the shifts, looking for a mattress or a sleeping bag and a quiet spot to grab a few hours' sleep, there is time for more personal, "civilian" conversations. "Where are you from? What do you do in everyday life? Do you know this person or that?" And the big question that occupies us all: Why are we doing this? What brings someone to put everything on hold and report for reserve duty?

And I ask myself: So much time, energy, money, adrenalin, and mainly human life are invested in this huge military machine. If this existential national imperative, to be strong and defend our country, drives us to invest such enormous energies and resources then couldn't we allocate similar resources for a cause that is no less critical, one that would yield truly promising and substantial fruits—the challenge of making peace?

Shalom or "peace" is one of the most frequently used words in Hebrew. We refer to it daily, sing about it in songs, and pray for it at least three times a day. The word appears everywhere. Yet the meaning of *shalom* is not so simple. When I asked a friend for his definition of peace, he tentatively suggested "the opposite of war." The Wikipedia definition is "the absence of hostility" or "a relationship that is operating harmoniously without violent conflict." Other sites gave similar definitions. It appears that peace is often described more in negative terms (absence of war) than in positive ones (how good it would be if there was peace).

Between "war" and "peace," the former is more familiar and perhaps even more natural and obvious. Already in the Book of Genesis, we encounter plenty of violent conflicts. Even in modern times, it seems that there are people and countries that opt for conflict and war much more readily than they are willing to pursue peace, almost as if violence and war are ingrained in human nature. Peace is identified as a lofty ideal, as a goal that is to be sought after but is ultimately unachievable—a dream of the naïve. Often it even seems that the people expressing the old clichés like

"Israel is striving for peace" don't even believe the words they are saying.

Consider the following:

Are we devoting sufficient commitment, passion, energies, and resources toward achieving peace? And what if Israeli society and its policy makers dedicated themselves to peacemaking—both within the country and with its neighbors—with all the spiritual and material resources available? Would peace still be unattainable? **And what if the work of peacemaking became profitable, trendy, and fashionable, replete with advertising, promotion, and marketing campaigns?** Wouldn't there be more people, attention, and resources devoted to the direction of making peace?

War and violent conflicts are not simply motivated by human nature but also (and some would claim mainly) driven by vested interests of power, influence, and resources. **Yet what are the vested interests that drive peace** that would motivate people, communities, societies, and organizations to dedicate the best of their efforts and abilities to this cause?

And what does peace look like? What color, taste, and smell does it have? Thanks to the images of war and violence that we are bombarded with, such as live broadcasts and printed media, movies, games, books, advertisements, and more, we can all describe war, even those who haven't experienced it firsthand. Can we imagine and visualize peace in such a tangible way?

And what about the term "peace"? Is it too clichéd and pathetic? Has the time come to adopt a new term, a different word that would express that same lofty ideal and perhaps even mobilize us to achieve it?

But back to reserve duty. The radios sputter, the combination of hard work, sweat, fatigue, and adrenalin are at new heights as the war game extracts every bit of energy from the dedicated reservists, who represent many Israelis serving on military reserve duty, in order to prepare for possible war. And I wonder, **will it ever be possible to recruit, equip, and engage an army of peace?**

December 2010

CAN MIGHT AND PEACE LIVE TOGETHER?

After returning from reserve duty last December, I was inspired to write an article addressing the challenge of how to turn peace into something more exciting, engaging, and fashionable. In that article, entitled "Peace Duty," I raised a number of questions:

Assuming that a state of peace between individuals, communities, and peoples is an ideal situation that serves basic human needs such as survival, health, nutrition, and protection then why are so many physical and emotional resources invested in preparing for and making war while so little are invested in making peace? Can the answer be found in the "prisoner's dilemma," taken from game theory? In that scenario, while cooperation to achieve peace better serves the interests of the sides on both (or more) sides of the conflict, and even though they both are aware of the advantages inherent in direct cooperation, the players choose a strategy of non-cooperation and getting ahead at the other's expense, out of the suspicion that the other side will adopt the same approach. Is this a matter of human nature? Perhaps violent, oppositional, non-compromising behavior is more natural to human beings?

And if this is a matter of human nature then could this be the reason that the experience of war and violent conflict (as it is expressed in films, games, books, mythology, etc.) stimulates and excites us so much while peace is conceived to be pathetic, banal, and dull? Has anyone ever seen a child playing computer games that are oriented toward achieving peace?

As a result of that last article, I received many fascinating responses. I thank everyone who took the trouble to share with me their thoughts and insights on the subject of peace. Most of the responses I received could be divided into two main camps:

A. Many of the readers of my article focused on the Arab-Israeli conflict. The prevailing sentiment was that the chance for peace between Israel and its Arab neighbors is remote, and this is not because the people of Israel don't want peace but because the Arabs are determined to gradually take over all of the land of Israel, and, thus, no compromise or resolution is possible between the peoples. Many of those who responded to the article claimed that **making movement toward peace sends a message of weakness that the other side can take advantage of for its own gain.**

B. The second line of reasoning was that the chances to transform our world into one that is more harmonious and oriented toward peace are almost nil. **Human nature leans toward war and violence and not to peacemaking and compromise.** War and violent conflict play a critical part in a person's identity. People need to identify with a group that is "good," which is opposed to an opposing "bad" enemy, in order to define themselves. In short, they argued, peace is contrary to human nature.

According to these assumptions, any situation of peace is temporary and against human nature, problematic, boring, and depressing. With this disheartening prospect, I looked for other insights from the world of martial arts. Perhaps there I could find an answer to the question of how power, courage, willingness to fight, and determination to go to war can coexist with mutual respect, pursuit of peace, and a desire to avoid violent conflict. In short, **can the mighty and the peaceful exist side by side?**

In karate, the Japanese martial art, not only is there not a contradiction between force and avoiding aggressive conflict, but the values of karate and traditional martial arts actually call for the integration of force on the one hand and preventing violent conflict on the other, all while protecting the honor of the opponent. According to the value system of karate, **the most exalted victory is not subduing the enemy but avoiding a battle entirely.**

Gichin Funakoshi, founder of modern karate, in his book *Twenty Guiding Principles of Karate*, connects between the world of karate and the challenges a person faces when trying to achieve a full, secure, and satisfying life. The first three principles that Funakoshi describes in concise and clear Japanese style are the obligation to integrate between lethal force in training to kill an opponent with one's bare hands and an uncompromising attempt to prevent violent conflict while committing one's self to honor and justice.

According to the first principle of Funakoshi: **"Karate begins and ends with 'Rei' (respect)."** In karate there is no contradiction between the obligation to honor one's enemy, grounded in a strict moral code, and the motivation to overcome him in a battle, using defensive and offensive techniques, both physical and psychological. In karate competitions, after the traditional bowing to one another, expressing mutual respect and the commitment to the values of karate, the two opponents move to a position of fighting and, at the sign of the judge, begin combat, where they use their hands and feet as weapons. Immediately following the fight, the opponents return to face each other, bow in respect, and signal that the fight is over and honor is maintained.

An Arab saying goes, "If you push a cat into a corner, it will turn into a tiger." Disrespecting and holding one's enemy in contempt offers no advantage and reflects weakness and a lack of confidence. According to karate, it is imperative to honor and esteem one's opponent yet, even so, in the event of danger, also strike or even kill if push comes to shove and that is the only remaining option.

"Never strike first in karate" is the second basic principle: karate is intended first and foremost for self-defense. In the first lesson in martial arts, the karate student commits to using his abilities only for positive purposes. Almost paradoxically, the purpose of martial arts is to achieve peace.

When people hear about my involvement in karate, they almost always comment, "It's dangerous to be next to you." And I always clarify their misconception. Those who practice karate (and other martial arts disciplines) and are committed to its values are the least dangerous people. A true karate practitioner will not use his skills for a bad cause. He/she will choose the path of peace and avoid violent conflict as long as he/she can.

And now to our neighbors. Israel has always taken pride in its commitment to going to war only if it has to. War in self-defense. It's no coincidence that our army is named the Israel Defense

Forces. When it went into wars "of choice" (for example, the First and Second Lebanon Wars), Israel became mired in the Lebanese mud, and its citizens and soldiers lost faith in the ability of the army and the government to protect them. **In the commitment of war only as a last resort and only for self-defense, there is tremendous power, beyond the moral strength.**

"Karate stands on the side of justice" is the third principle. There are those who claim that "in the Middle East, there is no alternative; you have to 'play dirty' because the accepted norms of behavior don't work." I am convinced that this approach is rooted in weakness, both moral and physical. This doesn't mean that we can never take firm and even cruel steps to protect our security. Yet it has to be done only when there is no other choice and only in a way that is honorable and moral.

In conclusion, not only can you be right and even mighty and determined. **Without power there can't be righteousness and, without righteousness, power is diminished.** This is the integration of peace and power that strengthens each side. There is no need to go as far as Japanese martial arts. The principles appear in the Jewish texts, as it is written in the Book of Psalms: "G-d will give might to His people; G-d will bless His people with peace."

This week I came back from a business trip to North America. It was a long trip. With my biological clock out of synch, on the third night after my return I was still unable to fall asleep. A combination of intense jetlag and troubling thoughts. Even the karate practice earlier in the evening, followed by a beer, didn't help.

That night, after tossing and turning for long hours, I went down the hall and peeked into my youngest daughter Sivan's room. With the thoughts on this article still in my mind, I had a realization. I'm not the only one. There are millions of fathers in the world (and it's usually fathers that cause wars, not mothers) who are out there somewhere, in homes, tents, or under the stars, contemplating their children and mulling over the next day, their livelihood, health, and security, and driven by the desire to secure for their families a better and more secure future.

And I wondered if in the basic instinct of fathers there are two principles: to be strong and determined to protect their loved ones and, at the same time, to pursue peace to ensure their security? And if so, **can might and peace exist together?**

January 2011

EXODUS

At the Ben-Gurion Duty-Free store, about to catch a business flight to Canada, I purchased the movie *Exodus*. Watching movies, snuggled up on the couch with my children, is one of my favorite activities. Not only is watching movies fun, but some classics are based on significant moments in the history of Israel, and I believe that children can learn history more naturally by watching a movie than by sitting in class.

Exodus is one of those classics. At that time, the outside world thought very highly of Israel, and Israelis themselves firmly believed that they had "right" on their side. Since then our image has gone steadily downhill, so it is refreshing—comforting, even—to remember a time when it was obvious who were the "good guys" and who the "bad guys"; and we were the "good guys," with the right to a state of our own.

As I approached my fortieth birthday, I was warned by older friends that after forty the memory starts to go. Unfortunately, they were correct. On the other hand, one of the few advantages of a poor memory is the experience of watching a movie again and enjoying it all afresh. It would be hard not to enjoy watching Paul Newman play Ari Ben Canaan, the man who, along with his beautiful sister Jordana, his non-Jewish blond American lover, Kitty, and other pioneers, demonstrated decisiveness and determination, heroism and sacrifice—all with poise, beauty, and that Hollywood razzle-dazzle.

We do not need a blue-eyed Paul Newman or a Hollywood movie about the most significant chapter in the recent history of our people in order to feel emotional about the establishment of Israel. We are talking about a true miracle here. From almost complete annihilation, after suffering methodical murder and destruction, then overcoming the hard hearts and cold shoulders of most of the world—under unimaginable circumstances, against all odds—the Jews established a state of their own in their historical homeland then defended it from enemies who outnumbered them many times over, and finally turned that state into a thriving island of democracy. If that is not a modern miracle then what is?

Watching this long movie, my children were struggling to understand the chronology and follow the plot. As I answered their questions, I began to draw an unavoidable comparison between the desire of the Jewish people for a state and the similar desire of the Palestinian people. That is an uncomfortable comparison for a Jewish-Zionist to draw. In fact, it is more than uncomfortable. It is distressing and downright disturbing. I readily concede that the comparison is not perfect, and the two cases have many differences. Nevertheless, it is a comparison that is difficult to ignore.

First, let us consider the differences:

Unlike the Jewish people, whose roots go back thousands of years to the Patriarch Abraham and the Land of Israel, there has never existed a historical "Palestinian people"—"the Palestinian people" is an invention of the twentieth century, and it came into existence largely **because** of the Israeli occupation, not **in spite of** it.

Unlike the State of Israel, which is the only place on earth where Jews have their own country, there are many Arab and Muslim countries in the world that could have given the Arab-Muslim Palestinians a home.

Unlike the State of Israel, which rose out of the ashes of the Holocaust just a few years after the annihilation of millions of European Jews, those who now call themselves "Palestinian" never accepted the right of the Jews to their own nation-state. In 1947, they fiercely opposed the Partition Plan, and in 1948 they attacked the Jewish Yishuv in Israel—and lost.

Unlike the Jewish people, who asked only for the right to a state of their own in a tiny corner of the Middle East and had no expansionist ambitions on the neighboring states, the Palestinian leadership, for the most part, wants to overrun the entire Jewish State and wipe it off the map.

Unlike the State of Israel, which has created, from scratch, an island of prosperity and progress in the midst of a maelstrom of misery, the Palestinians have, until recently, focused on perpetuating that misery and demanding help from outsiders.

Unlike the Jewish Yishuv, which aspired to become a people in the homeland that had been ruled for generations by foreign invaders and various empires, the Palestinians aspire to establish a state **in place of** the Jewish one.

And the most significant difference of all: the Jewish State is "us," **and the Palestinians are "them."** One of the phrases I remember most clearly from my kindergarten days in the kibbutz is, "It's not fair!" Since those days I have learned, sometimes the hard way, that "life isn't always fair."

But the bottom line is over 1.5 million human beings who are not citizens of any Arab country, who live in territories that Israel rule, who define themselves as Palestinians, and who live under an occupying power with limited rights yearn for independence. Recently they have started to use methods that are more and more reminiscent of those used by Israel's founders, as I realized while I watched *Exodus*.

Some of those methods are:

Establishing national institutions and building the infrastructure necessary to establish a state: At the Herzliya Conference about eighteen months ago, I listened to Salam Fayyad, the Palestinian prime minister, who spoke after one of the senior ministers of Israel. After hearing both speeches, I had the feeling that most of the audience would have actually preferred Fayyad to represent them and not the Israeli minister. Fayyad presented, clearly and calmly, his vision for the institutions, processes, and culture of transparency that would form the infrastructure of a future Palestinian State. And this is what is happening in practice; even if the Palestinians do not unilaterally declare a State of Palestine in September 2011, it is obvious to anyone watching that they are doing what they can to establish a state.

Engaging everyone in the struggle: One of the most moving chapters in the establishment of Israel is the absorption of the illegal immigrants who, having survived the horrors of Europe, made their way however they could to the shores of the Promised Land. I remember hearing stories from Yishuv veterans of hundreds of legal residents who went down to the beach to mingle with the newly landed illegals to prevent the British authorities from identifying the illegals. Israel was not established by individuals but by the entire people. One of my saddest experiences as a young officer during the First Intifada in 1987 was the sight of hundreds of Palestinian villagers who blocked roads, participated in demonstrations, and threw rocks at us—the occupying army. I thought of the founding generation of Israel, of the mass struggle...only this time I was on the less heroic side of the barricade. Ever since the First Intifada, it has been clear that the Palestinian uprising is not a phenomenon of a few individual extremists but of the whole society.

Mobilizing the support of the world community: The methods are completely different, but the principles are the same. What Jewish leaders such as Chaim Weizmann once did via messages, letters, and sea trips, Palestinian lobbyists and their supporters now do via digital media, online journalism, and social networks. In universities across the world, the Palestinians are gaining support for their goals among the future leaders of the Western world. The November 1947 declaration in the UN General Assembly establishing a Jewish state in the Land of Israel was the culmination of efforts to mobilize public opinion. The Palestinians, after several wasted decades of using terror and violence to gain legitimacy, now understand the power of non-violent protest and public pressure on governments and decision-makers, and plan to use that power to gain a UN General Assembly resolution for their own state.

Overcoming differences in support of a common goal: *Exodus* described the divisions between the Haganah and the Lehi, a group that advocated violent struggle and acts of terror against the British. The Yishuv was divided about the best way to deal with the British and the Arab residents of the area. But the common goal—the establishment of a Jewish state—united the different factions of the Yishuv in the 1940s and led to a remarkable achievement: overcoming seven Arab armies and establishing a state. The Palestinians have only recently managed to join forces officially and in principle (and it is still too soon to tell how long that will last) as part of their efforts to achieve a state.

Using the weapons of the weak: In one of my strategy classes in Officer Training School, victory in battle was defined as "conquering territory and destroying the enemy." As the world becomes "flatter" and methods of communication become more sophisticated, information is transmitted across the entire globe in real time, and the emphasis has moved from conquering territory to conquering public opinion. When the exodus was intercepted and the refugees on board were not allowed to land in Israel, they declared a hunger strike and broadcast their struggle to the world using a primitive radio. The case last year of the *Mavi Marmara* is just one example of a military success that was a public opinion failure, a battle that the Palestinians and their supporters won by wielding the weapons of the weak. The popular uprisings in the Arab world in the last six months demonstrate the power of the weak, and the Palestinians will certainly continue to use these weapons.

In early 1988, at the height of the First Intifada, the Israeli leadership was struggling to respond to this unexpected and puzzling popular uprising. The commanders of my tank battalion asked me to be interviewed by foreign journalists. The First Intifada was a very challenging time for us, both professionally and ethically. We were combat soldiers trained to fight, but we were contending with women and children who cursed us and threw rocks and bottles at us. What could I say to a foreign journalist who, seeing a combat soldier facing a young boy, is sure he knows which is the "bad guy" and which the "good guy"—and, in his eyes, the "good guy" is certainly not the combat soldier.

When I spoke to the American journalists, I tried to be loyal to the truth and my values while also making my modest contribution to Israel's public opinion struggle. I told them, "We Israelis are good at being David but poor at being Goliath."

I believe that is still true today, with one small but critical difference:

In 1988, the Palestinians were not Goliath, but they were also not David. I hope they will never be Goliath, but step by step they are learning to be David.

June 2011

YOU'RE ALSO RIGHT

There is a well-known story about a rabbi who was called upon to settle a dispute between two of his followers. The first man poured out his complaints to the rabbi, and when he finished, the rabbi said, "You're right." Then it was the second one's turn. When he finished, the rabbi said, "You're also right." The rabbi's wife, who had been listening to the conversation, said incredulously to her husband, "What do you mean, 'You're also right'? They can't **both** be right!" The rabbi thought for a few moments and then replied, "You know, my dear, you're also right."

If an alien were to land in our general vicinity, his response to the Israeli-Palestinian conflict would probably be like that of the rabbi in the story: you're both right.

The Palestinian people are right when they expect and demand independence. The Palestinian father is right to long for a life in which he can sleep safe at home without fearing a midnight pounding on his door. The Palestinian woman is right to want to go from place to place without having to go through security checkpoints or risk arrest.

The Jewish people were also right when they returned to their homeland after a two-thousand-year exile, establishing their own national home. Jews are right to fear hatred and persecution, right to believe that only by relying on their own resources can they prevent the nightmare of another Holocaust. Jews are right to state that they are entitled to all they have achieved through their own efforts. The Jewish people are correct when they point out that the world has totally unreasonable expectations of them, expectations that are never imposed on any other people. And they are also right to fear that if they give away some of their land today then tomorrow the Palestinians might demand it all.

Friends and neighbors may say, "Why do you, the grandson of a refugee from Germany, offspring of kibbutz founders, army officer, and member of a religious community in the Galilee feel the need to justify the position of our enemies?" I reply, "I don't have to justify anything, but I **do** have to understand." It is not hard to find untruths, gross exaggerations, and significant holes in the Palestinian version of the conflict. But even the most extreme among us cannot deny that Palestinians lack freedom, live in very difficult conditions, declare themselves to be a people, and are hungry for independence.

In the '90s I believed, along with many others, that we could find a way to live side by side. We had the feeling that it was beginning to happen, that it would come to pass soon. I remember that I was even somewhat concerned, during my MA studies in Boston, that peace would break out before I could return to Israel. What would we only give to be able to have such concerns nowadays!

YOU'RE ALSO RIGHT

The speeches of Binyamin Netanyahu and Mahmoud Abbas at the UN General Assembly might have been the last nails in the coffin of the dream of living side by side—if not actually in peace then at least living without war. But this does not seem possible any time in the foreseeable future. Both speeches focused on why I am right/fearful/angry/threatened and why the other side is threatening/thieving/untrustworthy. From their own perspectives, they were both right. And with "right" like that, who needs "wrong"?

October 2011

FOR WE HELD PEACE IN OUR HANDS

During these trying times, when the thunder of warfare and the explosion of bomb charges threaten to obliterate the memory of the days of dialogue and mutual hopes, we must remember that we held peace in our hands. Peace is not a document or a far-off mountain peak that one climbs in order to place a flag on the summit. Peace is a path that allows people and nations to confront differences of opinion, culture, religion, and worldview. We are the students of Israeli and Palestinian schools that have met with one another, the Israeli and Palestinian businessmen that jointly established factories, the poets, athletes, clerics, and nature lovers. We are those thousands of people who, during the wonderful years of the 1990s, established new relationships between people and nations. We were the peace.

The last eighteen months have set the process of building the peace back generations. The return to the peace process will be long and full of hurdles, but we who touched the peace are the best reminders that the path still exists and can be walked upon.

Every day of every year, we are obligated to "tell it to the children." We must tell our sons and daughters, and perhaps our grandsons and granddaughters, that this is the way, that it is possible, and that it is not some mirage in the distance.

Our situation is like that of the survivors of a shipwreck that have somehow made their way to a deserted island and are trying to light a fire with some flint in order to ward off the horrible cold. After innumerable attempts, they succeed in lighting a weak flame, which does not catch the other pieces of wood and is extinguished after a few moments. Even though the flame has died out, those that saw the light and felt the warmth will continue endlessly to try to relight it until they succeed in seeing it burn, and it becomes a huge, warm, roaring fire.

We, who held the peace in our hands, will remember its feel, will speak of it to our children, and will continue to believe that it is possible. Because of that, the fire of peace will continue to burn.

April 2002

IMMIGRANTS

On an El Al flight to Toronto, passengers are awakened toward the end of the long flight with a boring breakfast that always reminds me of army meals. While chewing the greasy El Al omelet, I started a polite conversation with the woman sitting next to me.

Her name was Sigal Barak, and she was on her way back to Toronto after a working visit to Israel. Sigal told me about her job: giving advice and assistance to Israelis wanting to immigrate to Canada. My curiosity was immediately piqued.

According to Sigal, in recent years the number of Israelis immigrating to Canada has increased significantly, to the tune of hundreds of families a year. Most of the immigrants are in their thirties and forties, and they come mainly from the center of the country and further south; very few are from the Galilee.

"Why are the numbers increasing?" I wondered. "After all, Israel hasn't had a significant war in recent years, and our economic situation isn't that bad compared with the rest of the world."

"I think there are three main reasons," she said. "The general feeling of insecurity, the fear of a nuclear Iran, and—witness the social protests and the call for social justice—financial difficulties and the resulting frustration and bitterness. Many of the Israelis who are going to Canada just feel that their country doesn't take proper care of its people.

"Moving to another country isn't an easy thing to do," continued Sigal. "You need to be very strongly motivated. When I'm in Israel meeting families who are considering moving to Canada, I hear things like, 'For the price of a used car in Israel, I could buy a new car in Canada and still have money left over.' I hear the hopelessness and frustration that impels parents with children to take the drastic step of uprooting their families."

The communities that Israelis find the most attractive are Toronto in the east and Vancouver in the west. But Israelis also go to smaller Canadian communities, many of which actively recruit Israelis, particularly immigrants from the FSU who originally moved to Israel but are willing to leave it for the "promised land" of Canada. These smaller communities, such as Halifax in the Maritimes, are aging and in danger of disappearing entirely as their young people move to the larger cities. They view the Israeli immigrants as vital new blood. Sometimes these newcomers are even needed to make up the *minyan* (prayer quorum) in the local synagogue.

So Canada has turned into the promised land of Israeli Jews. People who have never even visited Canada chose to move there because of its reputation as a country that takes good care of its citizens. In contrast to tiny Israel, there are vast spaces in Canada. If you were to drop Israel into the middle of one of Canada's forests, you would never find it again. The flourishing Toronto community, which has become one of the leading Jewish communities in North America, is a warm and friendly environment for Israelis. Sigal said, "You can walk around my neighborhood and get by talking only Hebrew."

About six months ago I visited my friend Mitch Bellman, president and CEO of the Jewish Federation of Ottawa. When I landed in Canada's capital, Mitch invited me to go with him to a meeting of the Ottawa city council. The meeting was to discuss objections to the proposal to name the new city archives and library after the former mayor Charlotte Whitton, who in the late 1930s had lobbied to keep hundreds of Jewish orphans out of Canada. At the meeting I became a witness to a dark chapter in Canada's history, of which many Canadians are now deeply ashamed. Canada refused to open its gates to European Jews trying to escape their fate, as described in *None Is Too Many*, the 1982 book by Irving Abella and Harold Troper. The book's title was the response of a Canadian immigration agent who had been asked how many Jews should be allowed in Canada after the war.

Truth to tell, apart from the harsh winter weather, Canada is a very good place to live, with pleasant people, natural beauty, and a flourishing economy. I love Canada and Canadians. Nevertheless, it is heartbreaking to think that in less than seven decades we have the absurd situation in which Canada, a country that slammed its doors in the face of Jews fleeing the Holocaust, has turned into the promised land of Israelis.

November 2011

THE ZIONIST SOUL

This past week, I spent a few days in Cleveland. I have an especially warm place in my heart for Cleveland's Jewish community and feel very much at home there. For five years I worked closely with this community, building economic, social, and educational connections between them and the region of Beit Shean as part of the Partnership 2000 program. It was the leaders of Cleveland's Jewish community who recruited me to lead the partnership, initiating my return to Israel in 1998, after living with my family for several years in Boston.

Just as in many communities in the US today, the Jewish community of Cleveland is experiencing difficult times. The migration of young people out of the city, the abandonment of businesses from the city center, and a plunge in the donations that represent the lifeline for Jewish institutions are just some of the challenges the community is facing.

Among my meetings in Cleveland, I was able to have a heart-to-heart talk with my friend Chuck Ratner in his office at Terminal

Tower in the city center. Chuck is chairman of the board of Forest City, a family-led real-estate development company. For several generations, the Ratner family has been and remains one of the principal supporters of the Jewish community and of Israel, and its members can be found among the economic and philanthropic leadership. Chuck told me how my uncle Pinchas Sapir would sit on the couch in his home and not budge until he'd gotten his father to commit to another investment—to establish another factory in the periphery or finance another plan to create new jobs in the fledgling Israel of the 1960s.

Chuck Ratner is distinguished by several characteristics that make people like him so rare, and if only they could be cloned, the Jewish people and the State of Israel would be in much better shape. Among these are a heart as broad and towering as his office building, profound wisdom, the persuasive powers to lead others to acts of "tikkun olam," modesty and warmth, along with a total commitment to the perpetuation of the Jewish people and their future in the State of Israel.

Toward the end of our meeting, as we were about to part, Chuck admitted that he sometimes feels guilty that, in spite of his deep commitment to and actions on behalf of the State of Israel, he doesn't actually live in the country and doesn't feel that he is at the "front line" in Israel's struggles. I put down my bag, sat down again, and shared some thoughts of mine on this subject.

First, I believe that Israel is the best place for a Jew to live. Not just because it is our Jewish nation, where we are a determining majority and where Jews do not have to be an apologetic minority. Not even because, after two thousand years and only the second time in our people's history, there is a sovereign Jewish nation for the Jewish people. For me, the reasons also include the things that are more connected to the land, like the food, the climate, the landscapes, and the culture, the grand and the mundane.

Obviously, I am not objective, since I was born in Israel, and this is what I am used to (despite having lived abroad for several years). Yet, on the other hand, what is objective in this world? My wife and I like to joke that our house stands on the best piece of land in the Jewish world, since Israel is the best place for Jews, the Galilee is the most beautiful part of Israel, our community of Hoshaya is the optimal community in the Galilee, and our home is set facing the most beautiful view in Hoshaya.

Secondly, and particularly in our twenty-first-century world that is continually becoming more global and "flatter," the ability to live in one part of the world and be influential and involved in another part is becoming more and more prevalent. People like Chuck and his friends, who not only donate money but also contribute tirelessly to different organizations that support Israeli causes (i.e., public diplomacy, immigration, lobbying, higher education), represent a critical element in the worldwide system that is reinforcing and securing Israel's future.

The truth must be told. And so, ultimately, when missiles are falling and bombs are exploding, those who actually live in Israel are in the eye of the storm, and their children are those who sleep in shelters, are wounded, and suffer from trauma. Still, if we want to take a relevant example, even in the army, only a small percentage of soldiers are physically present at the front lines and actually take part in the fighting. Most of the armed forces (intelligence, maintenance, computers, etc.) is backing up, supporting, and enabling the fighting to take place without directly participating.

Could the army function without its backup forces? Clearly not. And can the State of Israel hold its own against the many fronts of the global world without the Jewish communities of the Diaspora at its side? Perhaps, but without a doubt less successfully.

And thirdly, and perhaps most importantly, the true problem is that most of the world's Jews don't support and assist Israel! An increasing percentage of Jews do not identify themselves with the Jewish state, don't visit, don't act in its defense, and don't see the connection with it as a source of pride that should be stated out loud. A decreasing percentage of Diaspora Jews recognize the connection between the independent existence of Israel and the fact that they themselves can live freely as Jews with equal rights in (almost) any place on earth. Today, the commitment to and support of the State of Israel are integral parts of the DNA of every Jew wherever they are. Thus, those who do stand at Israel's side should be honored, acknowledged, encouraged, and embraced, as at the same time we strengthen the connection and solidarity between the Jews of the world and their national home.

And so, for the Chuck Ratners of the Jewish world, please know that you are essential and perhaps even indispensible to the future of the State of Israel. I hope I'll be proved wrong, but I suspect that in the not too distant future we'll be needing you more than ever.

April 2011

SOLIDARITY

While walking briskly in Manhattan from one meeting to another, I recalled the first time that I visited New York, more than twenty years ago. Coming out of Grand Central Station with Betsy, my future wife, I was startled by the sight of so many people rushing along the sidewalks. I felt as if the crowd was heading directly for me, and I grabbed Betsy's hand and pulled her aside so we wouldn't get trampled. That summer I had gone from walking in the avocado groves of Kibbutz Ramat Yochanan to walking along the crowded sidewalks of Manhattan, and I found the huge change to be rather overwhelming.

Manhattan in the middle of July is full of life and tourists—and is hot, humid, and sweaty. Years later, even after dozens of visits to the city, I still get a thrill from the pace, the crowd, the rush, and the energy.

On my most recent visit to New York, I met my friend K. He is a businessman who has been active in the Jewish Zionist world in many roles, both high-profile and behind-the-scenes, and is a generous and devoted supporter of Israel. K. usually enjoys challenging me with complex questions about Israel, trends in Israeli society, and issues of peace and war. But this time I was the one who challenged him. The question I posed was certainly provocative, but, unfortunately, the scenario on which it was based is not totally hypothetical. "Let us assume for a moment," I said, "that Iran announces (and proves) that it has developed nuclear weapons that can reach Israel. It then issues an ultimatum: if, within thirty days, Israel does not meet Iran's conditions (conditions that Israel cannot ever meet, such as unilateral withdrawal from Judea and Samaria and the release of all Palestinian prisoners), Iran will attack Israel with nuclear-armed missiles."

Then I got to the question itself: "During the thirty days until the Iranian ultimatum runs out, how many Jews from the United States will get on a plane to Israel to stand with Israelis—not just with their hearts and wallets but physically—thereby putting public pressure on the US government to support Israel and use its position as the world's only superpower for Israel's sake?"

K. did not hesitate, and his unequivocal answer shocked me: "Twenty people or fifteen…maybe fewer." After a moment's thought, he took a deep breath and explained. "In nineteen forty-eight, more would have come. In nineteen sixty-seven, more would certainly have come but now not many." He continued, his voice becoming defiant, "Where was the Israeli public when the 'who is a Jew' issue was being considered, and a significant portion of US Jews were almost disenfranchised? How many Israelis really care about us here in the States? Are Diaspora Jews only needed for their money and influence? Most of the young Jews in the States don't identify with Israel and don't feel connected to it."

A few days after this conversation, when I was back home in the Galilee, we hosted two teenage American boys who are in the Bronfman Fellowship program with my eldest son, Guy. American participants in this program come from the elite of American Jewish youth and are chosen from hundreds of candidates via a rigorous selection process. I presented my provocative question to them, and once again I was surprised by the emphatic nature of their responses. One boy explained earnestly that in order to ensure the continuity of the Jewish people, it was vital for there to be enough Jews living outside of Israel in case Israel was wiped out. The other explained that the physical presence of American Jews in Israel would be less effective in pressuring the US government than demonstrations in Washington and threatening to stop Jewish donations to members of Congress.

This is a message I am hearing from more and more friends in the US, Canada, Britain, and Scandinavia. Furthermore, my friends are people who, for the most part, care about Israel, support it, and come to visit—and they are a minority. The number of people who feel connected to Israel is going down all the time. Overall, Israel is slowly losing the Jewish people, and the Jewish people are losing Israel.

The issue of the relationship between the Jews of the Diaspora and Israel is complex and has been studied by many. It seems that we can learn a few lessons from my conversation with K. in New York.

First of all, let us pray that we never need to find out what would happen in such a horrifying scenario, which, sadly, is certainly not entirely hypothetical. The scenario is so terrifying that most people prefer to ignore it.

Secondly, we must never, ever neglect our best friends outside of Israel's borders—the Jews of the Diaspora. There are those who claim that Israel is now strong enough not to need the help of Diaspora Jews. I believe this is an error. History is full of rises and falls. Although we are strong today, yesterday we were not, and who knows what tomorrow may bring? Israel makes great efforts, including financial, to secure friends around the world. We must do everything we can to guard and strengthen our bond with our brethren overseas, including exposing Israeli youth to the complexities of life in the Diaspora and the difficulties of maintaining one's Jewish identity outside of Israel. The Jewish identity of Israeli youth will only be strengthened by such exposure.

Thirdly, and notwithstanding the above, at the moment of truth, it appears that we Israelis will have to rely primarily on ourselves. I once researched the issue of American aid to Israel during the 1973 Yom Kippur War. The aid did arrive eventually and was a significant factor during the campaign, but it arrived very late and only as the result of great pressure on the US government. The US has many interests in our region, and they do not always coincide precisely with Israel's.

To return to the provocative question, I shared my thoughts with my fourteen-year-old daughter, Eden, and she raised another point to consider: not only would few Jews leave the Diaspora to come to Israel during our hour of need, but many Israelis are liable to leave Israel for a safer place for themselves and their families.

May we never need to find out the answer to this question.

July 2011

WHILE FACING THE GREAT SYNAGOGUE OF BUDAPEST

The Great Synagogue of Budapest was built about 150 years ago. With pews for three thousand, it is the biggest, most ornate synagogue in all of Europe, its grandiose appearance resembling a cathedral more than a synagogue. Today it is a tourist site and a reminder of the glorious past of the Hungarian Jewish community.

My family and I went to Hungary for the Sukkot holiday. We wanted a vacation spot that was not too far away, not too expensive, with pleasant weather, and where we could spend an enjoyable week together.

We devoted our first day in Budapest, on the eve of the festival, to learning about the city's Jewish heritage. We started out at Chabad House, where we made reservations for meals during Sukkot and then we walked a little further up the street to the Great Synagogue of Budapest. The Great Synagogue has many claims to fame, including being the synagogue where Theodore Herzl, the visionary of the State of Israel, had his bar mitzvah. Alongside the synagogue itself is the cemetery where a small number of murdered Jews of the Budapest ghetto are interred in mass graves, low mounds in the fenced graveyard.

Next to the synagogue, built on land where Herzl's house once stood, is the Jewish Museum. This unpretentious little institution contains mostly Judaica from the Hungarian Jewish community. At the end of the small museum is a room with photos and relics of the Budapest ghetto and the 600,000 Jews whom the Nazis exterminated during their efforts to wipe out the Jewish population of Hungary.

I moved slowly among the pictures of bodies in mass graves and of trains on their way to the death camps, every so often glancing at my children to see how they were reacting to this difficult exhibit. One cannot ignore the contrast between the beautiful, vibrant city outside the building and the horrific role the city played some seventy years ago. My happiness of the morning was replaced by a somber sadness.

After visiting the Jewish Museum, we continued our walking tour of the city. We crossed the Danube, the river that divides "Buda" from "Pest," and went up Buda Castle Hill to get a panoramic view of the city. But the museum continued to cast its shadow over me the entire time, on the hill, on our way back to the hotel, and all during our preparations for the festival that evening.

We dressed in our holiday finery, lit the festival candles, and hurried to the synagogue at Chabad House for Sukkot services. As I listened to the prayer leader's repetition of the Amidah, I found myself looking out the window onto the busy street below, seeking out the Great Synagogue of Budapest. Then the realization hit me like a shock: I, a Jewish Israeli, a father of four, a tourist, was praying across the street from a visible reminder of the past glory of the Hungarian Jewish community. I was struck anew by the wonderful miracle that is the existence of Israel. Israel rose from the ashes of the concentration camps and death camps, the ghettos and countless other hellholes. The survivors became pioneers and helped establish Israel—a free, sovereign, prosperous country.

My thoughts continued to wander, from the miracle to the growing numbers of Jews around the world who are alienated from Israel, who do not identify with it, who emphasize only its many faults and failings, who ignore the historical miracle that it represents and the fact that it is a source of pride, the basis for belonging, and a safe refuge for all Jews everywhere in the world.

I thought: the terrible past is still fresh and real, its horrors still recounted by eyewitnesses. It is not just the past that is so threatening—the future does not feel secure. Hatred and persecution of Jews still exist, and have in fact increased in recent years.

Even if the "real Israel" often falls short of being the "ideal Israel," even if it is not a perfect society, even if it is tainted with the same human failings that plague every other country in the world—corruption, egoism, hardheartedness, mistreating the "other"—this does not negate the fact that Israel is "the Jewish State of all the Jews." Even the Torah, beginning with the stories of Adam and Eve, Cain and Abel, the patriarchs, acknowledges that our world contains not just love and fraternity, but also lies, jealously, murder, and fraud. All Jews, whoever they may be, should feel connected to Israel and feel the country is connected to them. It is perfectly legitimate to criticize, to try to improve things, even to complain, but it must be as a supporter and partner and not as one trying to delegitimize Israel's very existence.

Some of my friends believe that only those who live in Israel have the right to criticize it. I disagree and declare that the Jews of the Diaspora have the right—nay, the duty—to criticize. But the criticism must come from a place of belonging, of a feeling that we share the same fate, and from a willingness to contribute and build together.

The Great Synagogue of Budapest is just one more reminder of the historical process in which we play our part. Although Israel is a miracle, it is "a miracle in progress," with no guarantee that it will last forever. A people without its own state are weaker and more vulnerable, more at risk of persecution and attack. Without Israel, without a piece of real estate to call our own, a place where we live as sovereign beings and not at the whim of others, the Jewish people will once again be weak, persecuted, and vulnerable. All Jews must feel committed and connected to Israel and must work to continue the miracle.

October 2011

HOLOCAUST? REMIND ME, PLEASE...

"**H**olocaust? Could you please remind me…" said Madeline with an embarrassed smile. "It's been such a long time since I took history in school, I don't remember what 'the Holocaust' was."

Stockholm, Sweden. The calendar declared that spring had officially arrived in Scandinavia, but the City of Islands greeted me with snow and rain, not spring sunshine. My friend Alter Saks was running late for our meeting, so while I waited for him at his office I took the opportunity to chat with Madeline and Stanislav, members of his staff. When they heard I came from Israel, they wanted to hear firsthand about my famed country. Instead of delivering a lecture, I asked, "When you hear the word 'Israel,' what's the first thing that springs to mind?"

Madeline (about forty years old, with a college BA), started out diplomatically: "Israel…ahhh, reminds me of history, something old, heritage."

Stanislav (of Russian descent, about thirty years old, with several academic degrees) was more direct: "Strong army, separation wall, lots of enemies."

And so we quickly came to the central question: why do the Jews and Arabs fight each other all the time? Madeline asked, "How come Israel can't make room for everyone?" She added, "Do the Arabs really want to kill you or do they just want the land for themselves?" I tried to understand the difference between her two alternatives and answered with a question: "Let us suppose they 'just' want the land for themselves. Would the six million Jews who would have to leave the country be invited to stay in Sweden?"

Madeline asked, "So why do the Arabs want to kick you out of there?" and I tried to explain. As background, I mentioned Holocaust Remembrance Day, which had taken place just the previous day. Madeline did not understand the word "Holocaust"! I was staggered to learn that a mere seventy years after the event, an educated woman, living in the capital city of an enlightened Scandinavian country, did not know what the Holocaust was.

An Arab proverb says, "He came to seduce her, but he blinded her." Stanislav tried to come to my rescue and explain what the Holocaust was, but his "explanation" left me even more horrified. He started out by "clarifying" that there are many questions about the Holocaust. How many Jews were really killed? Did it even happen at all? Why should the Holocaust in Europe mean that the State of Israel had to be established in the heart of the Arab world?

When I got back to my hotel, as a kind of sequel to my disturbing encounter with such ignorance about the Holocaust, I found an email from my friend Miki Nevo. To mark Holocaust Day he had sent me something he had written about a decade earlier, during a visit to Poland as the head of a delegation from the school where he was the principal. In this passage, my tough Sabra friend eulogized his family members:

"I came here to beg your forgiveness: forgiveness for not wanting to know for many years; for wanting to run away and not face it; for not knowing how to come to terms with it, nor how to understand it. Then I screwed up my courage and dared to visit. For not having the strength to encompass it; for not being able to alleviate it; for choosing to ignore the look in my parents' eyes; for hardening my heart to your great suffering: Please forgive me; please forgive me."

Holocaust Remembrance Day demonstrates the national consensus about the obligation to fulfill the commandment of "you shall tell it to your children" regarding the horrors of the Holocaust. There is no disputing the supreme importance of passing on the torch of history from generation to generation and of the urgency of the task. For time is passing, and soon there will no longer remain any survivors to tell of the horrors they experienced firsthand.

Together with the obligation to remember and to tell others, there is also no escaping the obligation to contend with the challenging question: what next?

After all, only three generations have passed, and yet the world is already repressing (at best) or denying (at worst) that the Holocaust happened. By the time three more generations have passed, the Holocaust will become simply another chapter in the horrifying history of the world, proving once more that there is no limit to the bestiality and cruelty of the human species—nor to the ease with which people forget.

In Israel, we need to agree on a new narrative and define another justification for Israel's existence, over and above the trauma of the Holocaust and our fear of its recurrence. We are also obliged to contend with the growing criticism from the world around us, when we are no longer shielded by the armor of the Holocaust that protected us for a few decades but is now rapidly rusting away.

Our new narrative should relate more to **what we want to be** and less to **what we are afraid will happen again**. In other words, we would do better to concern ourselves less with "the entire world is against us," even if that is true to some degree. Instead, we should focus more on the question of what kind of country we aspire to be: in our behavior toward the weak and the stranger, to the environment and nature, and to the enormous challenge of being "the chosen people" when sometimes, in our heart of hearts, some of us just wish to be like everyone else.

April 2012

SO MUCH CAN BE LEARNED FROM CHILDREN

So much can be learned from children. It was my good fortune to study negotiation and conflict resolution with some of the world's leading experts, but much of what I know about interests and their influence on decision-making in negotiation, and how to face challenges and threats, I learned from my children.

Recently I tried to understand the principle of interests from my nine-year-old daughter, Eden, and my seven-year-old son, Ari. I asked Ari, "Which would you prefer: to get one candy and Eden would get three or that neither one of you would get any?" "That's easy," he replied. "Better that neither of us would get any." I tried again. "What would you choose: that Eden would get one piece of chocolate and you would get two or that you would get four pieces and Eden would get five?" "That I would get two pieces," my seven-year-old responded decisively.

Twelve years ago I completed my undergraduate studies in Middle Eastern history at the University of Haifa and was accepted as a graduate student at the Center for Middle Eastern Studies at Harvard University. I arrived at Harvard fresh off of a kibbutz, with my wife, Betsy, and our six-month-old baby, Guy. We had no money to speak of, but I was full of motivation to succeed in my studies at the pinnacle of the academic world, to take advantage of the opportunity to learn from the world's finest minds, and to understand what had been troubling me for as long as I could remember: can the conflict in the Middle East be solved and, if so, how?

In my first month of studies, in the fall of 1994, I met with my academic counselor, Professor M. After a few words of introduction, this pleasant Jewish woman (who later went on to become a good friend) asked me what I intended to research during my studies. "I have a theory I would like to investigate," I replied. "I believe that, unlike other regimes and societies, the Muslim extremists won't be deterred by loss of life in exchange for inflicting damage on Jews, and extreme Muslim regimes, like that of Iran, for example, won't mind paying an extremely heavy price, including massive civilian casualties, in order to inflict a serious strike on Israel. This," I concluded, "creates an existential conflict for Israel, since, at a national level, Israel's (unofficial) nuclear deterrence capability is ineffective against an enemy that is willing to absorb such a heavy price. Furthermore, the traditional deterrent of capital punishment won't work with someone who is ready to sacrifice his or her life."

I finished speaking and took a deep breath. Professor M. looked at me with affectionate humor and said, "An interesting theory but too naïve. Give a few months to your studies and see what you think after that. Your time at Harvard will help you understand."

Unfortunately, I did not research my theory. I studied intensively, but as much as I learned, I became more and more aware of how elusive it all was. Even today I don't know if and how the conflict in this region can be resolved...

The use of suicide in the arsenal of terror, defying traditional approaches of deterrence, has become a worldwide phenomenon and the ultimate weapon for the weak. The nuclear technology that Iran is slowly acquiring is about to become the number-one existential threat to the State of Israel, placing Israel's long-term future in question.

The Katyusha missile attacks on Northern Israel during the summer of 2006 struck about a third of the country and practically shut down the economy of the region over a five-week period. The sector hardest hit was tourism. And yet, by the Sukkot holidays, only two months after the ceasefire, it looked as if life had returned to normal: the Galilee was full of tourists, the national parks overflowing with visitors, over five thousand visitors came to the *Hakhel* Festival of Jewish Culture at Tel Hai College, the hotels and bed and breakfasts were full to capacity, and the roads were clogged with traffic. This seemed to evidence the endurance of the northern front and the proud, Zionistic spirit that insists on restoring life to its regular routine.

Still, the speedy, almost compulsive return to normalcy is dangerous for Israel. The war of the summer of 2006 was a wake-up call and warning shot to the Jewish people in Zion. It reminded us what we should never forget, even without a war—that when you are surrounded by millions of enemies, who might prefer your destruction over their own wellbeing, you should be constantly on your guard. As many from the north took refuge in the center or south of the country, the weak and helpless were left in the bomb shelters—stark evidence of the deepening social and economic gaps in our society, which impair our ability to cope with outside threats. We saw that the IDF is not invincible and that, as the values of our society shift, even the army of the people is not immune.

The pessimistic doomsayers in Israel are increasingly heard in public debate. The country hasn't even celebrated its sixtieth birthday, yet more and more people are questioning the feasibility of its long-term existence.

When our daughter Eden had a hard time learning how to skip rope and was concerned about an upcoming rope-skipping test at school, we told her, "Acknowledge that this is hard for you, practice longer and harder than anyone else, and that's how you'll learn to skip rope." Eden understood, made up her mind, and set to work. After long hours of practice and blisters on her feet, today she is an excellent rope skipper.

The bad news about the existence and future of the State of Israel is that the threat is indeed real; as it is said, "If you are paranoid, that doesn't mean they aren't plotting against you." The good news is that the future is still in our hands, and if we understand, decide, and put our will into action, we will succeed. So much can be learned from children...

October 2006

TOURNAMENT OF WAR

Your entire body cries out for oxygen. Your heart pounds wildly in your chest. Your head is spinning, and your eyes struggle to focus on the target. You can barely lift your arms, and your legs are glued to the ground. Every second feels like an hour, and every fiber of your being aches for the whistle that marks the end of the fight.

A tournament karate match lasts two minutes. One hundred and twenty seconds of kicks and punches, blocks, fakes, and escapes. With total concentration, you must understand the moves of the opponent. All of your abilities and skills, the results of endless hours of training and practice, your physical ability and endurance, your personality and strength—all these are on the line as you face your opponent. All of you versus all of him.

One of the most important lessons I learned during years of practicing karate is the principle of "pouring water over the wall." This curious-sounding idea is taken from the story of Jerusalem during the Roman blockade. The besieged city was suffering from a severe drinking water shortage, yet the leaders instructed the population to wash their clothes then throw the washing water over the walls. This seemingly illogical act had a critical purpose—to mislead the Romans into believing that there was no lack of water and that they could continue their resistance indefinitely.

In a difficult karate match, applying the "pouring water over the wall" principle may tip the scales. Even as your energy is all but depleted, give your opponent the impression that you can keep on fighting as long as necessary to win. At this critical moment, you need to kick harder, block faster, and keep your eyes fixed steadily on those of your opponent.

Israel and the Hezbollah have been locked in combat for the past three weeks. Even though the Israel Defense Forces are superior in terms of numbers and equipment, the Hezbollah is cleverly exploiting the advantages of guerilla fighting. In this conflict, the IDF is the proverbial Goliath, although in our times, unlike the Bible story, David does not always triumph.

The present conflict has many long-range implications for the State of Israel. It will influence the routines of our lives after the fighting ceases, our economy, the character and structure of our army, and our ability to carry out operations that will change the borders of the country. It will also influence Israel's external outlook—our deterrence capabilities, the character of future conflicts with other enemies, our status in the world, our ability to attract Jews from the Diaspora, and, above all, our chances to survive in the long term in a hostile, heavily armed environment.

We can, and must, regard the coming days as the last seconds in a karate tournament. In spite of the heavy price paid, the difficult burden on the citizens living in the area of conflict, and the discrepancy between our expectations of a swift victory and the actual outcome, Israel needs to rally all of its strength—military and civilian alike—to emerge victorious. We must hit harder, block faster, and, above all, not flinch.

August 2006

SO, WHAT SHOULD WE DO?

"*The ultimate aim of Karate lies not in victory nor defeat, but in the perfection of the character of its participants.*" *(Gichin Funakoshi,* The 20 Guiding Principles of Karate*)*

So, what should we do? This question has been cropping up again and again among the Israeli and Jewish public over the recent months. Except for some isolated optimistic declarations by a few politicians, the consensus is pretty much clear: the State of Israel is in danger, and the situation is only getting worse. Not that everything was rosy in the past, but there is one obvious difference today: when the State of Israel was strong and its enemies believed it was weak, that was only half the problem. When Israel was weak and its enemies believed it was strong, that was also half the problem. Today the situation is much more dangerous: Israel is getting weaker, and its enemies recognize it.

That was the bad news. But there is good news as well. The better news is that, first of all, it is still not too late to divert from this dangerous course and, second, the key to this change is found within, inside Israel and not outside of it. The discussions regarding the future of Israel focus almost exclusively on the relationship with foreign entities, mainly with the Palestinians and Iran. I believe that the key to Israel's long-term existence is found in its ability to deal with the internal challenges, and the question to be asked is: "So, what should WE do?"

In the following, I have listed, in shortened form, ten main challenges that, if they are met successfully, provide answers to the question "So, what should we do?"

The first: To understand that the situation is indeed dire and we are facing an emergency situation. When a person is in a dangerous situation, he or she discovers tremendous resources of power, far beyond what they ever realized they possess (for example, the courage and physical power a mother rallies to rescue her child from a burning house). Unlike other periods in our nation's short history, in Israel and the Jewish world today, the realization that Israel is indeed in existential danger has not yet penetrated our consciousness. Contributing to this situation is the fact the dangers are perceived only gradually—first, intifada then the rise of Hamas to power, the war in Iraq and its consequences, followed by the war in Lebanon, while all the time in the background there is the global rise in radical Islam, the crisis of trust in the top echelons of the Israeli government, and the ever more realistic danger of nuclear weapons coming into the hands of terrorists and sworn enemies... The time has come to push that imaginary emergency button and announce: "Ladies and gentlemen, we are in an emergency situation, and we must organize accordingly."

The second: To be willing to pay the price. Recognizing we are in an emergency situation, and approaching life in Israel as in a country in danger, exacts a steep price. Because who would like to come and live in or visit a place that is declared "dangerous"? The priorities in life also change when an emergency situation is declared. We can no longer focus on the normal elements of life: work, children, entertainment, health. A state of emergency also entails anxiety and fear and could even lead to large sectors of the population leaving the country. I remember well the dilemma my wife and I faced during the war this past summer: how do we explain to our children that, in spite of the real danger that a katyusha missile could fall on our house, we were not going to leave our home for a safer place?

One of the largest challenges that Israel must face with its external enemies, as with the Palestinians, for example, is they are willing to pay an even higher price in the conflict and hold out under the most difficult conditions over extended periods of time, while Israel is less and less willing to do the same. This was particularly obvious during the war of the summer of 2006, when many citizens of the north abandoned the region (mainly those who had the means to do so) after the missile attacks started and the extreme sensitivity of the civilian public over IDF losses, which, officers claimed, had a negative effect on the army's operational abilities. To face the existential threat, the Israeli people need to recognize the situation as it is and be willing to pay the price.

The third: To strengthen the weaker layers of society. Like a chain whose strength is dependent on its weakest link, the power of this society is dependent in large measure on its weakest layers. A society where the gap between the haves and have-nots is constantly growing, along with the percentage of people living under the poverty line, will not be able to remain strong in the face of existential crises.

The problem does not lie with the prosperity of the stronger sectors of society but in the gap that has developed between them and the weak. In an emergency, the entire society must enlist, and the price must be paid by everyone. It would be very difficult to recruit from the entire spectrum of society without a fundamental belief that this society is a just one. It is critical to reinforce public education, opportunities for employment, and the position and image of all layers of society, and to provide them with opportunities and resources, and not only government allocations and charity. One can imagine the positive influence of a campaign where, in response to the emergency situation, the fifty richest people in Israel will announce that they are contributing 30 billion shekels over the next five years in order to strengthen Israeli society and prepare it for the current and future challenges.

The fourth: To update the national system of values. In Israel's not too distant past, the national heroes came from the agricultural settlements, the army, and the schools. To be a farmer in the Negev or a high officer in the army was considered "elite." I remember the respect that the farmers and officers were given at the kibbutz where I grew up. To plow the fields at night on a giant tractor or to be an officer in a combat unit was considered the ultimate honor. Every child knew who the most senior officer on the kibbutz was and who was allowed to drive the largest John Deere tractor.

Our value system has gradually changed, and today it is not a disgrace not to enlist in the army at all, while the highest ambition is to sell a company. A country that is secure among its neighbors has the luxury to relegate army service to a peripheral function in society, and establishing a start-up can be the dream of any young person. At a certain point during the end of the last century, we dreamed that perhaps we had reached this stage. Apparently not. The State of Israel is still not there, and it is imperative that the country promote, acknowledge, and compensate (not only financially) those who are building and protecting it.

The fifth: To repair and reinforce the connection with the minorities in Israeli society. Throughout Israel's history, the young country has been occupied with absorbing new immigrants and the challenge of the relations between the majority and the minority. These were the immigrants from Northern Africa during the 1950s and the immigrants from Ethiopia and the FSU in the 1990s. In spite of the immense difficulties and many mistakes made along the way, Israel has succeeded in growing in size and strength by integrating these new members into society. Yet the State of Israel has still not succeeded in its connections with the Israeli Arab minority. In spite of the improvement in their standard of living, which is rising along with the rest of the country, and in spite of pronouncements made by successive prime ministers (remember the promise of 4 billion shekels made by the Barak government?), the frustration and bitterness among Israeli Arabs is growing. As Israel is conceived as weakened in specific sectors of the external world (the Hezbollah and Hamas), the extremist voices are being heard even more: calls for separatism and questions about the Jewish nature of the state, on the Arab side, and increasing declarations that Israeli Arabs are the enemy from within, on the side of the Jews.

Israeli Arabs are and can continue to be a national resource. They can bridge between us and our Arab neighbors and enrich us through their rich and varied culture, economy, and society. Changing our approach to the Arab Israeli minority from a burden to a resource is a top priority.

The sixth: To create and promote a common agenda with Diaspora Jews. In the global village we live in today, the time has come to transform the separation between Jews in Israel and the Diaspora and unite ourselves as the world Jewish people. We must build upon what we have in common, create a common language and agenda, and face our challenges together. For many years I have an ongoing argument with a friend of mine from the States who is one of the leaders among American Jewry. He insists that, since he doesn't live in Israel, he doesn't have the moral right to actively participate in determining its fate when it comes to questions of borders, deciding when to go to war, etc. And I claim that I see him as an important partner in determining Israel's course into the future. Both of us are right. I am convinced that we need to distance ourselves from questions of who needs whom more, Israel the Diaspora Jews or vice versa, and who has this or that moral right, and focus on the connection between Israeli and Diaspora Jews and their common fate, and, as such, galvanize the tremendous human and physical resources of the Jewish people to secure Israel's future.

The seventh: To agree upon and preserve the public values and ethics in Israel. It seems that, never in its history has the State of Israel had so many of its senior government figures under criminal investigation. Some say it is not that there is not more corruption today, but only more corruption is discovered. This may be true.

SO, WHAT SHOULD WE DO?

The important point is corruption in the highest places radiates downward to the ordinary citizen. Because if they (the leaders) can steal, molest, and be unfaithful then why shouldn't everyone else? If there is one thing that the average Israeli can't stand to be, it's a sucker ("friar"). So much corruption all around makes the average Israeli feel like perhaps he and his wife are the only ones who are playing by the rules.

One of the first rules they teach in IDF officer's school is that "officers eat after their soldiers." It is only befitting that this principle could be espoused by Israel's leaders as well.

The eighth: Appreciate, preserve, and protect our environment and natural resources. Despite its small size, the land of Israel is blessed with an incredible richness, beauty, and variety of landscapes. Within its borders lie a unique collection of snow and desert, canyons and mountains, seas and lakes. In addition to its awesome natural resources, Israel has more historical and cultural treasures per square meter than any other country in the world, with Jerusalem the hands-down leader.

Yet along with its natural and historical treasures, Israel is evidently the dirtiest country in the Western world. Every time I return from a trip to North America or Europe, I am amazed anew at the amount of garbage strewn across the Holy Land. Even the few beautiful rivers and streams flowing through the country are getting more and more polluted. Beautiful spots like Nahal Kziv and Nahal Amud, where, until not so long ago you could drink from their waters, are increasingly polluted by waste. In the past, the excuse of "security needs" was used to justify polluting our country: "What's the big deal for a country like Sweden to be clean? They don't have wars to fight. And when there's peace, then we can clean things up." If we continue waiting for peace, there won't be anything left to clean. Whoever doesn't protect the land, beaches, and waters of their country won't be able to protect their borders either.

The ninth: To unite around our religion and promote the beauty of Judaism as a cohesive factor. It has been said about the Torah of Israel that "[i]t is a tree of life for those who grasp it," and in the same breath, "Its ways are ways of pleasantness and all its paths are peace." It seems that each verse depends on the other. When we emphasize and focus on the beauty, sensitivity, and humanity in Judaism, it serves as a bridge between people and communities, and as a help in resolving disagreements and conflicts. Yet when the emphasis is on the extreme, the divisive, and the negation in the Torah, it is used as a tool among those who would sow discord and fraction among the Jewish people.

I believe that in the religion of the Jewish people lies the ultimate key for strengthening our people in the twenty-first century and for connecting between the communities in Israel and the Diaspora. There are several figures who are doing this faithfully and successfully, like Rav Bigman of Ma'ale Gilboa and others, not only religious Jews but also those who use religion as a bridge between hearts, as a connecting force. Unification around our religion will not only strengthen the Jewish people among ourselves but will also strengthen our position among the peoples of the world, including our Arab neighbors, who particularly value and admire faith.

The tenth: the personal challenge. Every person can make his or her own contribution to this effort. Every person who is concerned

SO, WHAT SHOULD WE DO?

about the fate of the State of Israel should ask him or herself what he or she can do for the future of this country.

The suggestions for action outlined here are a humble attempt to answer the question "So, what should we do?" What these suggestions have in common is that they are all internal affairs of the Jewish people or, in other words, are not dependent on what happens in Iran, Lebanon, in the Palestinian government, or even the United States. This doesn't mean that Israel should or could even allow itself to ignore what is taking place around it. Obviously not. The difference is in the focus. For decades, the public debate in Israel (like the political divide between left and right and the discussion over the future of the territories) centered around issues whose focus faces outward, to try to improve Israel's situation in relation to our neighbors. I propose that now is the time to improve ourselves.

December 2006

SOME SAY THAT CONTEMPORARY ISRAEL IS EUROPE OF THE 1930S ERA

Israel's Prime Minister Benjamin Netanyahu has been saying for a while, "We're living in nineteen thirty-eight, and Iran is Germany," as a way of highlighting the danger of a nuclear Iran. Now that Israel's treatment of and attitude toward foreigners in general and Arabs in particular is sharply declining, should we consider saying, "The time is now the 'thirties, and Israel is Europe"?

About six months ago, my family and I were visiting the Old City of Jerusalem. At the entrance of the Jewish quarter, my wife suddenly pointed to a small sign hanging on the glass door of a store selling Judaica. "Look at that, Sagi," she said, her voice a mixture of surprise and disgust. I went over to look. In black and white, the sign said, "Jewish store." The associations that came flooding into my mind deeply upset me. In the blink of an eye I traveled back eighty years to Germany in the '30s, remembering the stories I was told by my grandfather, Michael Benartzi, of blessed memory, of what he had experienced in the land of his birth before he managed to escape to the land of Israel.

I wanted my children to understand just how their mother and I felt about that sign, so I pushed open the glass door and strode into the store. As my children watched, I politely asked the saleswoman to explain the sign. I added, "Doesn't that remind you of Nazi-occupied Europe?" "What on earth do you mean?" she answered with a strong French accent. "It's important that passersby know that the people selling Judaica are Jewish and not Arab. There are Arabs who pretend to be Jews, you know." I thought about confronting her bigotry but in the end decided not to make a scene. We left the store and continued our way to the Western Wall, where I added one additional prayer to the many others that the majestic old stones heard from me that evening.

As month followed month, the phenomenon of arson attempts on mosques began to spread across Israel: in Jaffa, in Tuba-Zangriya, in Jerusalem. Israel police seem incapable of stopping this phenomenon. Jews burning houses of prayer? How long has it been since our own houses of prayer were burned in Europe and our holy books were dumped in a heap and set on fire? Have the Jews who behave this way today never heard of Kristallnacht? Are they truly ignorant of what we suffered that night in November 1938? As well as arson, we see harassment and attacks on Arab students in Safed, attempts to silence muezzins in mosques, boycotts of Arab labor, and other iniquities.

On my way to work one bright winter morning, I visited Mohammad Darawshe in his home in the Galilee village of Iksal, located in the northern end of the Jezreel Valley between Nazareth and Mount Tabor.

Mohammad, a highly educated and eloquent man, is co-executive director of The Abraham Fund (http://www.abrahamfund.org) and is well-versed in all aspects of coexistence. After exchanging some brief small talk, I asked him about the mood on the street among the Israeli Arab population, in the light of these incidents of racism and violence, both physical and verbal, against Israeli Arabs.

"People are worried," said Mohammad somberly. "There's uncertainty and fear. I no longer let my oldest son go to town with his friends; I think it's too dangerous for him. People are worried about the future, scared that they'll be kicked off their land, scared they'll lose the right to vote and will officially become second-class citizens.

"I tell my children," he continued, "that the only asset they have is their brains and their education. Who knows if one day they might have to leave behind all their property, their land, their home, and run away without anything other than the clothes on their backs? In that case the only thing we would be left with is our education and our abilities." Does that sound familiar?

I left Mohammad's village with my stomach churning. As if to add fuel to the fire, on my way to work I heard a radio report about mistreatment of migrant workers from Africa.

There is no doubt that we are in a protracted struggle for control of Israel. We are currently at the height of a historic struggle over territory, hegemony, resources—and the character of our country. But does this struggle require us, the Jews of Israel, to ignore Jewish values and universal values, the democratic principles on which the State of Israel was founded and which are included explicitly in our Declaration of Independence, and the religious laws commanding us to behave kindly to the strangers in our midst? Does such immoral, racist, discriminatory, degrading behavior strengthen Israel and improve its self-image, social cohesion, and chances of survival—or does it do the very opposite?

December 2011

ON THE KNIFE

According to a summery Arab saying, "*Fi ayam al-batikh, mafish tabikh*," "In watermelon season, no one cooks." On my way home one evening from a meeting, I decided to stop at a fruit and vegetable stand on the road through Kfar Manda to buy a watermelon for the Melamed family. My recent watermelon purchases at roadside stands had been somewhat less than successful. Too often, the promise of "honey watermelon" or "sweet and fresh" is no more dependable than chaff in the wind, vanishing as soon as the "green outside, red inside" orb is opened. Instead of sweet and refreshing, the flesh proves to be tart and pasty. Sadly, even the watermelon, that symbol of summertime refreshment and innocence, can pass its prime when exposed to the mercies of a blazing Israeli summer.

The traditional solution to the problem of buying a pig in a poke (or, rather, an unopened watermelon) is the rite of **al hasakin**—literally "on the knife"—during which the vendor creates a "window" through which the purchaser can judge the inner depths of the watermelon. Unlike buying mutual funds, where the risk is always borne by the investor, this rite is more akin to the tasting and approval of wine from a newly opened bottle at an expensive restaurant. When you and the vendor agree to *al ha-sakin,* the responsibility for the quality of the merchandise rests upon the vendor. According to the customs of *al ha-sakin,* the vendor, using a thin, sharp knife, cuts a narrow triangular wedge deep into the flesh of the watermelon and withdraws it using the tip of the knife stuck into the rind then presents the wedge—on the knife—to the purchaser for tasting and approval. And the most important rule is: if the watermelon is not good, the customer is under no obligation to buy.

The vendor at the rickety stand in Kfar Manda was very sure of himself when I asked to buy *al ha-sakin.* "Which one do you want?" he asked. "You choose," I replied. "You're the expert." Of course, that also meant he was responsible for picking the right watermelon and could not later claim I had simply made a bad choice.

The young vendor tapped several watermelons, listening to the dull sound echoing in their distended bellies, and eventually selected a dark, heavy watermelon. From under the table he drew out a long, sharp knife, sliced into the watermelon, withdrew a deep, narrow wedge, and presented it to me on the tip of his knife. I tasted it, enjoyed it, and gave my approval.

While my purchase was being bagged, I took the opportunity to dust off my rusty Arabic and catch up with the local news. "What's the story with the Sudanese here?" I asked, referring to the major altercation in Kfar Manda a couple of weeks earlier, between the locals and the Sudanese migrants living in the village.

One of the locals, also a customer, upon hearing my question, smiled grimly and shook her fist to signal her opinion of the relations between the local inhabitants and the so-called guests from Africa. The young man himself was actually more understanding. "They're hungry, they come here looking for work, they take whatever they can get. I feel sorry for them." Another young man, standing nearby, called me over and pointed out some industrial buildings set back a few hundred meters from the road. "You see those? Once upon a time they were chicken coops, dairy farms, factories. Now they're full of Sudanese. They sleep there, all of them together, then in the morning they go out looking for work."

With the watermelon in hand, I went back to the car deep in thought. Israel's treatment of migrant workers from Africa in some ways resembles the *al ha-sakin* test, creating a window that allows us to look deep into the heart of Israel in the twenty-first century.

First of all, the very situation reflects a great absurdity. The State of Israel, a country that was established less than a century ago as a refuge for the remnants of the Jewish people, that was recently ranked 150 out of 158 countries on the Global Peace Index *(http://www.visionofhumanity.org)*, that has been surrounded by enemies from the moment it was born to the present day—tiny Israel has somehow become the Promised Land and sanctuary for the miserable of Africa, who flock to its borders despite the immense difficulties of their trek.

Secondly, the migrant workers from Africa have created another link in the food chain that is the Israeli employment scene. When Israeli Jews no longer found it prosperous and prestigious to work in agriculture, the work was taken by Palestinians. When Palestinians were no longer permitted to work in Israel, Chinese and Thai workers came instead. Israeli Arabs are also becoming much choosier about the work they do, and this is where the Sudanese and Eritreans come in.

Today the African laborers are employed in Kfar Manda and other Arab villages in the area, doing the work that the villagers themselves are no longer willing to do. It is also interesting to remember, perhaps with nostalgia, the days—a mere hundred years ago—when the pioneers in the Zionist Movement fought for the right to do manual labor. The Zionist pioneers wanted to create the "new Jew" who would live by his hands, and they struggled with the landowners for the opportunity to work the land and support themselves by the sweat of their brows.

Thirdly, the attitude of the Israeli public to the migrant workers from Africa is nourished by two polar opposites. On the one hand, there is a deep fear of "the other" coupled with some naked bigotry and fear of their growing numbers, like KIng Pharaoh, who knew not Joseph: "Look, the Israelite people are much too numerous for us. Let us deal shrewdly with them, so that they may not increase; otherwise in the event of war they may join our enemies in fighting against us.'" (Exodus 1:9–10). On the other hand, Israelis have a strong instinct to help and to try to find a humanitarian way to deal with the issue. Many good people have been enlisted to the task, guided by pangs of conscience and the memories of the time, not so long ago, when it was the Jews who were the persecuted refugees, on the run and seeking asylum.

One way or another, at the height of another hot Israeli summer, Israeli society and its decision-makers have been charged with the responsibility to wrestle with yet another complex, multifaceted issue, an issue that will require a combination of determination and firmness, sensitivity and compassion, long-term vision—and a great deal of wisdom.

June 2012

CONNECTED?

We normally assume that the advanced technologies of the twenty-first century have improved communication between people. E-mail allows us to communicate immediately and inexpensively, and social networks enable us to create virtual communities, developing friendships across land and seas. Now it is so much easier to share information, dreams, and feelings with others. The cell phone enables us to stay in constant contact with others, friends, and loved ones anywhere in the world. And the list goes on.

But do advanced technologies really make us better communicators? Some insights I had from a family gathering brought into focus some of the questions that have been bothering me for some time now.

It was a beautiful blooming spring day in the Galilee, one of those days that invite you to step outdoors and breathe the fragrance of the blossoming trees. Nature was still at its finest, even though the shades of yellow were already visible in the landscape.

On that day, I was invited to attend a family gathering, celebrating one of the Israeli holidays. This social event brought together family members who don't regularly assemble in their full configuration, and there were representatives of three generations around the table. Grandparents, uncles and aunts, and grandchildren. A family event like this is an opportunity to bring ourselves up to date with what's new in the lives of each and every family member and even recount some bitter and sweet nostalgia.

Well into the holiday meal, after everyone at the table had satisfied their initial hunger, appetites whetted by the fresh spring Galilee air, they started into their second and third courses. At that point, I started to detect the negative effects of technology on our family interactions.

Three of the grandchildren gobbled their food, escaping from the table and into the house to sit in front of a computer screen and watch a cartoon. Another grandchild went off to a quiet corner to play a popular computer game and, with dramatic gestures, tossed virtual fruit across his cell phone screen. At the same time, one of the uncles settled back into his plastic chair, busy with his cell phone, his attention riveted to the little black device, trying to figure out a new bit of software.

When I tried several times, unsuccessfully, to get his attention, my daughter Eden suggested that I call him on the phone. "A very original idea," I answered her with a smile. And so, sitting at a distance of four feet from one another, I called his number. Only when he heard my voice through the loudspeaker of his telephone did he sit up in his chair and raise his eyes to look at me with an embarrassed grin.

So does advanced technology actually enable better communication between people? Does the technical ability to speak to and see people through electronic devices help us to listen, see, and hear each other better? Are a thousand "friends" on Facebook actually **friends**? I received my briefing on social networks from my kids. And when troubling questions began to arise, I shared them with my kids. "How many of your Facebook friends are truly your friends?" I asked. "And if you sent all your friends on the network a request to contribute ten shekels to help with a medical problem, G-d forbid, how many of them in your estimation would respond positively and send a donation?"

And further. Who among us hasn't found themselves at the dinner table with their family, after a long day of work/errands/school? Finally the family has all gathered together, after each one had been occupied with their daily concerns. This is the only opportunity in the day to talk, relate experiences, share, and listen. And suddenly someone's cell phone rings, a friend from work who remembered some open issue from the work day. I already answered the phone, and this unwelcome conversation, which could well have been postponed to the next day, takes our attention away from the closest and dearest thing. And while I'm trying to end this unnecessary intrusion, the children have already left the table and gone to their computer/homework/telephone, leaving us alone, with telephone in hand, but no one else around the table.

And perhaps the worst of all (at least for now—surely something worse will come along) are the smart phones. The little beep that announces that an e-mail has arrived. You may be in the middle of a romantic encounter with your wife, or a conversation with your child about what happened in school, or even just reading the evening paper…but your curiosity trumps your common sense and tempts you to peek at the little screen to read the freshly arrived mail, just to see that it is another advertisement for Viagra.

In our modern world, flooded with electronic temptations, Shabbat represents a kind of city of refuge. On observing Shabbat, it is said by our forefathers, that "more than the Jewish people take care of Shabbat, Shabbat takes care of the Jewish people." We were awarded with twenty-five hours, once a week, during which the action ceases, the television, the computer, the tablet, and the telephone are turned off, the iPhone and the BlackBerry, and all the rest of the "communication" devices that control our attention during the week, to make room for communication with one another and with ourselves. The transition isn't always easy, particularly for those who aren't used to it. On a recent Shabbat, we hosted friends who don't usually keep Shabbat. I asked the youngest child of the family, a cute eight-year-old, how he was experiencing Shabbat in Hoshaya. "Very nice," he said. "But I can't wait until it's over so I can check my messages on Facebook."

So do the communication technologies really improve our communication with our loved ones and ourselves or just seem to? Perhaps the advanced technologies aren't just friend but are also foe.

When you examine the amazing leap of communication technologies over the past twenty years, one can only imagine how significant the next technological leap will be in the years to come. Technological developments are driven (mainly) by economic considerations and the expectations of earning profits. No doubt the human abilities for concentration are not developing at the same pace. This may seem, perhaps, to be a radical comparison, but, in fact, gunpowder and the atom bomb were also developed to solve human challenges. More and more, it seems to me that one of the central challenges of the human species in the decades to come will be to develop sensibilities, sensitivities, and mechanisms of defense and protection against advanced communication technologies.

May 2011

EVERYTHING IS POLITICAL

"We are children of our age,
it's a political age.

All day long, all through the night,
all affairs–yours, ours, theirs–
are political affairs.

Whether you like it or not,
your genes have a political past,
your skin, a political cast,
your eyes, a political slant."

(*Children of Our Era* by Wislawa Szymborska, translated by Joanna Trzeciak)

A few years ago, we subscribed to the newspaper I shall refer to as *M1*. We had been looking for a paper that was not crammed with dicey photographs and sensational headlines, and for the lack of many other options, we decided to give *M1* a try. We quickly came to the conclusion it was not for us. Although the newspaper did not have nude photos or headlines about pop singers who expose themselves emotionally ("I started singing because my father beat me/my mother was an alcoholic/my brother came out of the closet/I ran out of drugs"), we felt its worldview and perspective were narrow and limited.

Ever since we canceled our subscription, sales agents occasionally phone to try to convince us to resume it. My oldest son, Guy, told me about a recent attempt.

"Hi, this is X, representative of the newspaper *M1*. May I speak with Mom or Dad?"

"My parents are not here. May I help you?"

"I'm calling about subscribing to the newspaper. When will they be back?"

Guy, knowing and sharing our attitude toward *M1*, decided to deal with the agent's call himself.

"You can talk to me. I'm empowered to make decisions about the household newspapers."

"I would like to offer you a subscription to the newspaper *M1* at a special introductory price in honor of the holidays."

"No, thank you. We already subscribe to *HA* and *G* [two other newspapers], and we don't need another one," said my son.

"You subscribe to *HA*? What? You support the enemy?"

My son responded immediately. "Leaving aside the political aspect, you have to agree that *HA* is a better quality newspaper than yours," he told the stunned sales agent.

"What's 'quality' about it? Have you gone over to the other side, reading the newspaper of the leftists?"

"It's okay," said my son. "We like to see the bigger picture, and *HA* helps us maintain a balance."

"'It's okay'? What do you mean, 'It's okay'! Soon you'll be completely brainwashed! You'll be like the Jew who wanted to see how the other half lives and ended up eating pork." By this point the hot-tempered sales agent had completely forgotten everything he learned in telemarketing school about listening to the customer, about the "soft sell," about not negating the potential customer's position. He treated my bewildered son and my innocent family—which, after all, had simply wanted to find a newspaper to read—as if we had deserted our country and run into the arms of the enemy.

Once upon a time I thought the function of a newspaper was to report objectively on what was happening in the country and around the world. When I grew up I understood that the concept "objective" does not really exist and that a newspaper will always reflect a certain worldview and philosophy. But where does it end? What have we come to when one's choice of reading matter is considered a political act, if not potentially treasonous?

October 2011

FROM PIONEERING LEADER TO MUSEUM EXHIBIT

In my senior year of high school I initiated and assembled a "construction work team," aiming to develop skills in the various building trades among new Israeli high school graduates and to prove that young Jews should also take an active part in construction work, which was then traditionally an Arab work sector. My idea and call for action to create a "construction work team" was also inspired by literary sources from the *Second and Third Aliya* (immigration to Israel) periods such as the writings of A.D. Gordon.

A.D. Gordon, the father of the "religion of labor," is synonymous with the ideal of "Hebrew labor," of conquering the Jewish homeland by physically working the land. A.D. set a personal example of the pioneering ethos. I wonder what he would have said if he could have seen his name appear on the stylish menu of the Café Rishonim (Founders Café) restaurant at Kibbutz Degania as

"Gordon Salad." Would he have thought of it as something negative and bourgeois or would he perhaps have considered it to be part of fulfilling his Zionist dream: the Jewish people living in the land of Israel and making its living from the land?

On *TuB'Av*, the Jewish "Day of Love," my family went canoeing on the Jordan River. To get there we drove to the entrance of Kibbutz Kinneret, next to the Christian baptismal site *Yardenit*, and then went down a dusty dirt road until we reached the "Rob Roy" compound, a place that aspires to be an Indian village and where one can rent canoes. We sat in the canoe and began to paddle in the last rays of sunlight, disturbing some blue red kingfishers that had already nested down for the night.

The Jordan River has something in common with the movie star Tom Cruise: the myth is larger than the reality. Tom Cruise on screen seems to be tall because he is handsome and an excellent actor, but in fact Cruise is a rather short man (not quite five-six). Similarly, a first-time visitor to the River Jordan comes with high expectations because of its mythic status but is liable to react to the reality with surprise: "What, that's all there is?!" The river is not wide, not deep, and not very full of water. Perhaps we expect more from the river the Israelites crossed on their way to the Promised Land and which played such an important role in early Christian history. But, still, the Jordan is the best river we have. It is a great pity that the hundreds of visitors along its banks do not take better care of it.

It was twilight by the time we finished canoeing. The children jumped from the canoe into the cool, greenish water and splashed around with great enjoyment. As all parents do, we had trouble getting them out of the water until I yelled, "We're going to eat at a restaurant!" That did the trick. Canoeing on the river had given us all a healthy appetite. We went from the legendary river to the restaurant at the legendary Kibbutz Degania, just a few minutes from the baptismal site.

Degania was the first kibbutz—the first in Israel and the first in the entire world. As such, it is called "The Mother of Kibbutzim." It was established in 1910 on the shores of the Kinneret (Sea of Galilee) by ten men and two women who were pioneers of the *Second Aliya*, an act that marked the start of the kibbutz movement. The founders of Degania wrote, "*On 25th Tishrei 5671, corresponding to 28th October 1910, we ten men and two women came to Umm Juni… We came to establish an independent settlement of Hebrew laborers on national land, a collective settlement with neither exploiters nor exploited—a commune!*"

The story of the first kibbutz is not the only one to adorn Degania. Generations of Israelis grew up on the legend from the 1948 War of Independence, of the Molotov cocktail that was thrown by a brave defender into the turret of the Syrian tank, stopping the Syrian army's advance and saving the Jordan Valley.

We parked and went out into the warm night air. The Café Rishonim restaurant is situated in the middle of the Founders Courtyard, several old buildings arranged in U-form with the courtyard in its center.

We sat down inside the restaurant, which opened a few years ago in one of the historical courtyard buildings. The floor tiles reveal the history of the place; they are black and brown spotted, as was the kibbutz tradition, and measure twenty by twenty centimeters. Such tiles are no longer seen very often. They are remnants from the days when the "*balata*" (tile) was simply a floor covering, not a pretentious artistic statement.

We glanced at the menu, which featured the founding heroes: "Bussel Salad," "Baratz Sandwich," and "Hayuta Health Salad" (I was pleased to see that the founding women were not forgotten). A century after they came to the harsh land and made it bloom, the pioneers of Degania have become food celebrities.

When my salad arrived, it was a perfectly seasoned kibbutz-style: olive oil, lemon, salt. The salad reminded me of the art of preparing and eating salad on kibbutz. After all, salad is the cornerstone and centerpiece of two of the daily meals, breakfast and supper, every single day of the year. The art and science of the salad has three components: chopping the ingredients to the correct size, the seasoning, and calculating the quantity of bread required to mop up the salad dressing. A kibbutznik who finishes the salad before the bread (or vice versa) has failed to calculate correctly and will have to get another slice of bread or chop up some more salad in order to correct the balance.

While mopping up the salad juices with the fresh bread of Café Rishonim, I thought about the way the first kibbutz in particular and the kibbutz movement in general has morphed from a revolutionary movement that changed the world under very trying conditions into a pastoral community on the banks of the Kinneret with a restaurant offering kosher dairy meals in a pleasant, air-conditioned location. This is a transition taking place before our very eyes, from spirited, trailblazing movement into a museum exhibit—a place where we come to wax nostalgic over what once was.

FROM PIONEERING LEADER TO MUSEUM EXHIBIT

In 1951, American professor Bruno Bettelheim came to Kibbutz Ramat Yochanan to research this new species of human being, the kibbutz children. His research was published in the controversial book *Children of the Dream*. A few years ago I heard one of the veterans of the kibbutz, whose childhood was one of those researched by Bettelheim, talk about the famous professor. "So this weird American professor came to our kibbutz. He didn't speak Hebrew; we didn't exactly understand his questions. We just fooled around and joked, and afterwards he wrote it all in a book…"

In recent years we have witnessed the growth of memoirs that describe kibbutz life from various viewpoints. It seems it is still too early to analyze the kibbutz movement and its accomplishments from a historical perspective. The subject is too loaded with subjectivity, nostalgia, and personal involvement.

As a third-generation child of kibbutz, a descendent of the founders of two kibbutzim, it is not easy for me to witness the process that is changing the kibbutz movement from part of our national story to something whose best days are now history.

We children of the kibbutz were brought up with the belief of being the chosen, the torch bearers leading the camp. But perhaps finding your place in history is not such a bad thing after all—it is the nature of history and the way of the world. Even the Roman Empire did not last forever.

The kibbutz will always have a special place in the history of the Jewish nation and the State of Israel. The important question then becomes: who in Israel will take the place of the kibbutz movement and be the new pioneer that leads the camp?

August 2011

MODESTY

The late Pinchas Sapir (née Kozlowski) was the brother of my late grandmother, Rachel Kozlowski, and when I was very young he would sometimes come to our kibbutz, Ramat Yohanan, to visit her. On one of Sapir's visits, I proudly told my fellow kindergarteners that he was Israel's finance minister, and that meant he was the richest man in the country because he controlled the finances of the entire State of Israel. But I must admit that I was at a loss to explain why Uncle Pinchas, even though he was the finance minister, lived in such a modest one-bedroom home in Kfar Saba.

Pinchas Sapir's character is well-illustrated by this story, told to me by Steve Stulman, who heard it from his friend Harold Hill of New York:

"It was in the 'sixties, during the time Pinchas Sapir was finance minister," related Harold, "and I was on a visit to Israel to examine some investments in the young Jewish state. Sapir and his wife, Shoshana, picked up my wife and me to drive us to their home in

Kfar Saba for dinner. While we were in the car, Sapir and Shoshana talked to each other in Hebrew, not realizing that I understood the language. 'Pinchas,' said Shoshana quietly, 'winter is coming, and the house will be cold. The old heater doesn't work anymore—we need to buy a new one.' 'Shoshana,' replied Pinchas, 'I'm not certain we can afford to buy a new heater this year…'"

Pinchas Sapir was uncompromising in his management of Israel's industry and economy, overseeing its development with a firm hand. He followed Israel's economy closely, without benefit of a laptop computer or smartphone, using only his famous black notebook and little paper notes. Everyone knew that a note from Sapir was more binding than a written legal document. Today such a management style would certainly be considered highly inappropriate, to put it mildly. But Sapir's modesty and ability to be satisfied with so little for himself were legendary, and it was clear that what drove him was his concern for the country, the urgent national requirement for economic development and job opportunities that would allow Israel to absorb waves of new immigrants. There was never the slightest suspicion that he had used his position for personal gain. Everyone knew that what he did, he did because he believed it to be the right thing, never because it profited himself or his relatives. This next story illustrates this quality very well:

At a recent book launch at Moadon Tzavta in Tel Aviv for a new biography of Pinchas Sapir by Michal Sapir (Pinchas's granddaughter), Michal's father, Amos, was asked about his mother, Shoshana. "My mother didn't have an easy life," related Amos. "Dad was rarely at home. Our mother coped with the financial challenges. Apart from raising the family more or less by herself, on the weekends she had to host many people at our home, and our financial resources were very limited. All her life she bought on installment plans... One of my mother's creative methods for dealing with the household finances was to sell the daily newspapers that Dad brought home to read to the fishmonger in Kfar Saba for a few pennies..."

Compare that with the situation today. Israel is currently facing a housing shortage, and it is becoming increasingly difficult for average Israelis to afford an apartment. Nevertheless, we recently learned that a senior minister in the government "in response to pressure from the public" had sold his ostentatious apartment in an exclusive tower complex in Tel Aviv for 26 million shekels and instead purchased a "smaller, more modest apartment" for a mere 8 million.

Deuteronomy (17:20) defines the behavior expected of the king: "Thus he will not act haughtily towards his fellows or deviate from the commandment to the right or to the left—that the days of his reign over the kingdom may be long." Humility and modesty are very powerful qualities for someone in public service, someone who aspires to be a leader. These qualities allow their possessors to lead and to be role models. While we do not want the wife of a government minister to have to sell old newspapers to the fishmonger to make ends meet, nevertheless a little humility and modesty in our leaders of today would certainly not come amiss.

March 2012

MONEY OR IDEAS?

"Do you want me to pay you with money or with ideas?" asked Professor Roger Fisher.

"I have a baby at home and have to pay twenty thousand dollars a year in tuition fees. Please pay me in cash, and I'll pick up the ideas as I go," I answered, having no idea that I was negotiating with the first person in the world to develop a universally applicable method of negotiation and from whom I would be given many ideas and concepts that were of inestimable.

Roger Fisher passed away this month at the age of ninety. Thousands of his students and colleagues remember his great influence on them while at the same time appreciating what Roger Fisher gave the world to make it saner, wiser, more logical. I had the privilege of having him as a professor and mentor and even was graced with the opportunity to work with him.

We first met in the winter of 1994, a few months after I arrived in Boston to study for my MA at Harvard. One evening, the head of the Center for Middle Eastern Studies, knowing I was in desperate need of additional income, suggested I meet with a professor on the faculty of the Harvard Law School. "His name's Roger Fisher, and he's a famous figure in the field of negotiations. He's looking for help with some research on the subject of the Middle East. You should meet him."

So one rainy evening I went to Fisher's office in Pound Hall, where he greeted me with a smile. At first I had trouble understanding his accent, as he leaned back in his chair with his hands behind his head and regaled me for about twenty minutes with stories of his adventures in global conflict resolution: Peru and Ecuador, Salvador, the USSR, South Africa, and more. After this exciting start, he sat up, looked me straight in the eye, and said, "The one conflict I haven't been involved in yet is the Israeli-Palestinian conflict. That's a challenge for me. Israel and the Palestinians are supposed to sign a permanent peace agreement in nineteen ninety-six, and I'd like to help them conduct fruitful negotiations. But I don't want to come across like a know-it-all American, giving advice to the natives. Go check for me what's going on in conflict resolution in the area…"

And that is how, as a research assistant and then as a student and disciple, my relationship with Roger Fisher began. It was also how I was introduced to the "principled negotiation," a subject first presented to the general public some thirty years ago in his famous book *Getting to Yes*. Even though it was published decades ago, this volume is still a world best-seller and has been translated into thirty-six languages.

Roger was a great believer in using a good story to convey a message, and he would spice his university classes with stories from his full life. One day I went up to him after class and asked, "Did all your stories really happen?" The celebrated professor just smiled and said, "These are always true stories as I tell them…"

Roger did not wait for conflict to come to him; he actively searched for them. With the help of two organizations he founded—CMG (a not-for-profit group) and CMI (a consulting firm)—he sought challenging conflicts the way a hunter stalks its prey. But the conflict that attracted him above all others was the one between us and our Palestinian neighbors. For him, it was like a missing jewel from the crown of his achievements. One day he asked me to introduce him to Professor Yair Hirschfeld, who was involved in the Israeli-Palestinian negotiations as one of the architects of the Oslo agreement and who had been one of my professors during my BA studies. "Please invite him to come to Boston as my guest at Harvard," Fisher told me. I contacted Yair, who said that while he would be delighted to meet Professor Fisher, he would only be in New York, and there was no way he could come to Boston at the moment. Declared Hirschfeld, "It's not negotiable!" I gave Yair's unequivocal answer to Roger, whose response was, "So he said, 'It's not negotiable'? Aha…" The esteemed professor looked like a child who had just been given a chocolate bar. "What if we tell Professor Hirschfeld that I just happen to be hosting President Clinton and his wife, Hillary, at Harvard, and I would be delighted if he could join us? Do you think he would still have said 'it's not negotiable'?"

But the most important lesson that I learned from Roger was the difference between **interests** and **positions**. A position is what one party to the negotiation **declares** is important to them. An interest is what is **truly important and critical** to them. This lesson has stayed with me everywhere I go, including in my family life.

During the period that I gave seminars on the theories of negotiation that Fisher developed, I would present the following example to illustrate the difference between a position and an interest: When my oldest son was a baby, my wife and I were arguing about who should put him in the car seat. Neither of us liked to do that. Then one day I asked Betsy, "What is it you don't like about putting Guy in the car seat?" "I hate having to deal with the buckle; it always gets stuck." "Ah," I said, "and the reason that **I** hate doing it is because when I bend to put our sweetie pie in the car seat, it hurts my back." After that, Betsy would put Guy in the car seat, and I would do up the buckle…

More than once I have found myself thinking, when faced with a complicated situation, *What would Roger have said?* Sometimes I would consult with him by phone. It was a privilege and a pleasure to get advice from the best. He was always an optimist. About ten years ago I was involved in cross-border collaboration with Jordan. I sent Roger material on the programs and asked for his advice. On June 12, 2002, he sent me back a letter that ended with these words: "The current political situation is certainly difficult. The only way I am able to maintain my optimism is by reminding myself that today there is more room for improvement in Palestinian-Israeli relations than anytime I can remember." I wonder what he would say today…

Dear Professor Fisher,

You are now ensconced in "the undiscovered country, from whose bourn no traveler returns." Perhaps it truly is a place of perfection, but I feel sure that even up above you will find conflicts to solve. But if there really are no conflicts there, please try to send a message and a few hints to help those of us down here.

Rest in peace.
Your student and admirer,
Sagi Melamed
August 2012

DAILY NEWSPAPER

Fifteen years ago, I was a graduate student in Boston, and, like most students and young couples, my wife and I lived frugally, scraping by from paycheck to paycheck. Two months after we arrived, my mother's cancer came out of remission, and during this difficult time, we became frequent international phone callers. Dialing Israel from the US was expensive at that time, more than $1.50 per minute. Our phone bills were large, to say the least.

While Bezeq (Israel's leading phone company) enjoyed an undisputed monopoly on the Israeli phone market, competition was fierce between phone companies in the US, with the customer being the direct beneficiary. Suddenly we were getting 'incentives' from competing phone companies. Checks for fifty to one hundred and fifty dollars arrived in the mail, attached to a letter saying, "Simply sign the gift check, deposit it into your account, and join our international phone service for a better price than the one you are currently paying." Simple. No strings attached.

And so I found myself, in my first year as a student, depositing a new check into my bank account every few weeks, a gift from a different long-distance phone company each time. Our budget enjoyed the occasional respite, and our international phone bills kept shrinking as our calls to Israel became more and more frequent.

I recalled this anecdote while I was subscribing to a daily newspaper. Our previous subscription had finished, and after a few weeks without it, I decided that reading the paper is important to the family. Especially to our son Ari, an avid sports fan. Each morning before breakfast he needs to read the results from the basketball and soccer games played the night before and update the family over breakfast. Even though you can find all of the news online, I am still an avid fan of a newspaper that you can hold in your hands and read as you lie on the carpet. It's also fun when your son runs over to you to show the scores and makes comparisons between players.

Two years ago I had a subscription to *Globes*, but I cancelled it since the rest of my family didn't find it interesting. Copies of the newspaper would pile up unopened during my frequent trips abroad, embarrassing my environmentally conscientious family. By coincidence, I received a call from a marketing agent by the name of Yossi Cohen. "We have decided to give you a free month's worth of newspapers," he announced. "Great!" I replied. And so we received a free full month of *Globes* delivered to our home. In the meantime, the kids kept reminding me that they had absolutely no interest in it. There were no sports pages, and they were bored with its business orientation. In the meantime I called *Ha'aretz*, my preferred newspaper and found that their monthly subscription was a pricey seventy dollars per month.

Once my month of free newspapers came to an end, I got another call from Yossi Cohen from *Globes*. "I'd like to interest you in a forty-dollar-per-month subscription." After a long chat we came to the conclusion that I wasn't interested, especially not at that price, but that he could call me again after Passover.

Immediately after Passover, he called again. At this point I realized that I was dealing with a top-notch telemarketer, one of the best in the business. It was almost impossible to say no to him. After he lowered the price so far down that I promised him that I wouldn't publish it, and he promised that the subscription would automatically expire after nine months, I gave in and signed up for a subscription to *Globes*.

On my way home from work that evening, I decided to retry *Ha'aretz*, and when I spoke to the marketing agent I made it clear to her that I would not consider paying a subscription greater than fifty dollars a month. Thirty minutes later she excitedly called me back with the message that I received a 50-percent discount, cleared by the supervisor, and so the cost of my monthly subscription would be thirty-five dollars a month. I was happy. This was the option I had initially preferred.

I arrived home and immediately called *Globes* to cancel the subscription that I had ordered only a few hours earlier, and they told me that I would get a call back from a representative within forty-eight hours.

Yossi from *Globes* called at 8:00 a.m. the next day. At this point I felt like I was speaking to a close friend. "What happened, Sagi?" he intimately asked. I tried to explain. Yossi wouldn't let me go.

"It's very important to us that you remain our client. I'd like to offer a few special gifts to change your mind."

To make a long story short, I finished the conversation with my *Globes* subscription intact and with several complimentary gifts, my need for which was unknown to me prior to the call. Truth be told, I could not say no to Yossi. I felt like a person walking hurriedly down the street but stopping to listen to a captivating street musician. The musician is playing. The music gently engages a passerby, who in return feels compelled to put his spare change in the musician's hat. I felt a real commitment to Yossi Cohen!

The lesson I got from *Globes*' Yossi Cohen about sales, determination, sticking to your goal, and being creative and at the same time the lesson I learned about the competition between daily newspapers and how the individual customer could use it to his/her advantage were so instructive and illuminating that I felt I had gotten my money's worth. And now the Melamed family has two daily newspapers.

May 2011

TO BE AN OFFICER

At the president's conference at the Binyanei Ha'Uma in Jerusalem, I ran into Hasson Hasson. When we last met twenty-five years ago, Hasson was a captain. Today he is a brigadier-general and serves as President Shimon Peres's military secretary.

Even there, among all the political and business movers and shakers of the world, Hasson Hasson stood out, just as I remembered him a generation ago at the officer training school north of Mitzpe Ramon in the Negev Desert. I saluted him with a smile. It took him a few moments to remember our last meeting, and then we hugged and agreed to get together soon.

Very early in my army career, I aspired to be an officer. After an intense year-long training course, I became a tank commander and was assigned the prestigious position of instructor in the tank commanders' course. I excelled there, too, and just *knew* I was destined to be an officer. After six months of instruction, with outstanding references in hand, I applied for the officer training course. To my shock, and to the surprise of my comrades and commanders, I failed the psychological test—twice. (In retrospect, perhaps it was because of my failed attempts to flirt with the attractive young psychologist who was examining me.)

I refused to abandon my dream of becoming an officer. Avigdor Kahalani, in his book *The Heights of Courage* (in Hebrew, *Oz 77*), describes how he was kicked out of officer training because of his supposed lack of command and control ability. He went on to serve as a platoon commander without becoming an officer and ended up being awarded the Distinguished Service Medal for his command of a tank platoon during the Six-Day War, followed by the Medal of Valor (Israel's highest award) for his conduct as commander of the 77th Battalion during the Yom Kippur War's fierce tank battles on the Golan Heights. The citation for the Medal of Valor, presented to him by then-Defense Minister Shimon Peres, read: "Lieutenant-Colonel Kahalani displayed remarkable leadership and personal courage in a difficult and complicated battle, one that changed the result of the Golan Heights battlefield."

I reasoned that if anyone would understand my dream, it would be Brigadier-General Kahalani. A young sergeant needs a lot of chutzpah to call a brigadier-general, but I did not lack for chutzpah. I called him at his home in Nes Tziyona and told him I wanted to be an officer. "Come to my house," said Kahalani in his military manner. So Saturday night I hitchhiked from my kibbutz to Nes Tsiyona. We sat in his neat living room as his wife, Dalia, graciously served us coffee. I said I had excelled throughout my military service, and I wanted to continue to excel as an officer. I added that he, more than anyone, should know that psychological tests do not always reflect the abilities of an officer. "I'll look into it," said Kahalani, as he brought our meeting to a close. Two weeks later

TO BE AN OFFICER

I was told to go to officers training school and join the course as a cadet.

I entered the officer training school in the winter of 1986. Temperatures in the Negev Desert can be deceptive. Although the days are usually warm, on winter nights it can become terribly cold. I remember how, during one night navigation exercise, I stood on the summit of a hill and unbuttoned my pants to relieve myself. It was so cold that my fingers froze, and I was unable to close my pants again, so I had to continue navigating with open pants. Only when the blood returned to my fingers could I finally do up the buttons.

The cold was the least of our challenges. The heavy study load, the training, the discipline, and the fear of getting kicked out of the course meant that the cadets had to be tough, focused, and self-disciplined.

My platoon commander at officer training school was Lieutenant Hasson Hasson, who had served in the Golani Brigade and came from the Druze village of Daliat El Carmel. We cadets liked Hasson on sight. He was a professional officer, devoted to his soldiers, with a modest manner. We also knew that as a Druze, in order to reach his current position he would have needed to work harder and be more professional and determined than his Jewish comrades.

About ten days before the end of the course, three other cadets and I were sent to a kibbutz in the north to write the company's graduation newsletter. This was a perk for cadets who had done well in the course and also had a talent for creative writing. When I returned to the base after that coveted journalism gig, it was already the eve of Rosh Hashanah. Our company had to stay behind to guard the base during the festival, and I was immediately assigned guard duty at the firing range about two miles from the main base. I marched to the firing range wearing my battle vest and weapons, and when I got there I sat down and opened the book that would help me pass the time.

After about two hours alone in the silent, peaceful desert, I suddenly noticed a small dust cloud approaching me. When the dust cleared, I saw the on-duty instructor standing in front of me. Seeing his angry face, I knew he had not run all the way to the firing range to bring me the traditional Rosh Hashanah apples and honey. "Why didn't you answer the radio? You abandoned your guard duty! You'll pay dearly for this!" he yelled at me. I had no idea what radio he meant. Today, twenty-five years after the fact, I now understand that he was yelling because he was scared of the trouble he had gotten himself into, since it was his responsibility to give me the right instructions for guard duty. But at the time I did not know that, and my heart sank. I did not answer. I finished my guard duty and went back to the base.

The day after the festival I was told I could go home for Yom Kippur and then, when I came back, I would face a court martial. My mood was as low as it could be. I was scared I would be kicked out of the course. I had gone to such lengths to get into the course and become an officer—and now to be kicked out over something so stupid? When I got home I asked the kibbutz hairdresser to shave my head in preparation for my expected arrest. And so I returned to the base.

It was the end of the officer training course. While my comrades practiced for the graduation ceremony, I waited to be court martialed. The day of the court martial I polished my shoes until they shone like mirrors. I straightened my cap and stationed myself at the office door of the battalion commander, Lieutenant-Colonel G. Lieutenant-Colonel G. was unusual in the army. A member of a moshav (cooperative farm), he had returned to the regular army at a relatively advanced age after many years as a civilian. Despite explicit orders to do up all one's shirt buttons, G. went around the base with his shirts unbuttoned at the top, refusing to set a personal example in an environment where setting a personal example was considered supremely important. We did not think particularly highly of him.

Accompanied by the instructor, I entered his office and saluted. He enumerated my crimes and asked for my reaction. "I made a mistake and am willing to pay the price," I answered quietly. I had expected to be kicked out of the course but was pleasantly surprised: although I was sentenced to three weeks in military prison, I was not kicked out. I was very happy that my wish had come true; I could continue my military career and complete the officer training course.

The next day I heard the cheers of the military choir greeting my comrades at the graduation ceremony. The base was full of delighted families giving their soldier offspring food and drink, admiring the officers' pins worn proudly on their lapels. All my friends were getting ready for the coveted week-long vacation at the end of the course. I, however, remained in my room and prepared to go to military prison. But despite that I was not upset at all. I had not been kicked out!

The next day the base emptied, leaving only me, some guards, and some clerks. No one said a word about prison. Instead, I was told to help the base's gardener put up the sukkah for the approaching Sukkot holiday. I also found some comfort with a woman soldier who had been unlucky enough to be assigned guard duty at the empty base. Paradoxically, it turned out to be one of the most beautiful weeks of my entire four years in the army. At the end of the week, I was told to report to Shizpon Base and join my comrades in the armored division officers course.

I had not seen Hasson Hasson since that time. When I would occasionally visit his village on the Carmel Mountain, I would ask after him and send my regards. I am convinced that he was the main reason I was not kicked out of the course and that my prison sentence was commuted to building a sukkah. And so, Brigadier-General Hasson, I dedicate this column to you, to your family, and to your past and future accomplishments.

With a salute,
First Lieutenant (res.) Sagi Melamed
June 2011

SON OF A KIBBUTZ—ASSETS AND LIABILITIES

Hatzerim Air Force Base. The ceremony where pilot training course graduates receive their ranks has just ended. My brother-in-law, who himself holds a high-ranking position at the base's school, invited us to come and see this impressive ceremony.

After the ceremony was over, we sat down together for a festive dinner on the porch of the military residence where my sister, brother-in-law, and their three children live. The air of the Negev Desert was hot and dry, even at this late evening hour. As we finished the meal, and when I was already contemplating the long road ahead of us back to our home in the Galilee, my brother-in-law said, "Tell me, did growing up on a kibbutz traumatized you too?" "What do you mean?" I asked. "Well," he answered, "when you think of your childhood on the kibbutz, what are the first thoughts that come to mind? Positive or negative?" I started to think. The truth is this was the first time this (very good) question had ever crossed my mind.

Some weeks later. Parents' summer camp at Hoshaya. Every child's parents are responsible for occupying and entertaining their children and their friends over one summer vacation day. Thanks to parents' camp, the families of Hoshaya manage to survive the long, hot vacation months and disconnect their kids from Facebook at least for a few hours. In our family, it was clear that the responsibility for this children's activity (which most of the year is my wife's jurisdiction) would fall on me. And if that was the case then it was obvious that my son and his friends would be going for a visit to the kibbutz I grew up on, Ramat Yochanan.

Ramat Yochanan is one of the oldest and most established kibbutzim in the Kibbutz Movement. It was established in 1932 by a group of immigrants mainly from Eastern Europe and soon established a position of strength and leadership among the other kibbutzim. Today, its economy relies on a factory that manufactures polycarbonate sheets, with millions of dollars in exports each year. Some call it the kibbutz that laid the plastic egg. Agriculture, which used to be the crowning glory of the kibbutz, is now practically only for show—to maintain control over the land and to occupy a few kibbutz members.

I was born into the third generation of the Melamed family on the kibbutz. My grandparents were among its founding members—not the first but among them. My grandfather was a kind of unique *kibbutznik*. One of the kibbutz elders who is no longer with us once told me, one afternoon in the avocado grove as we were harvesting the fruit, that my grandfather died of heart failure at a young age because of "hyper-activity."

SON OF A KIBBUTZ—ASSETS AND LIABILITIES

My father was born on Ramat Yochanan just a short time after the War of Independence, and his most vivid childhood memory was the evacuation of the children to the nearby town after an attack by the Druze on the kibbutz. My father is a classic product of the kibbutz. Highly talented and motivated, he, in spite of the senior positions he held and continues to hold at the kibbutz (today he is chairman of the kibbutz industries and chairman of the regional factories, among others) still cares what the dairy man said about him to the laundry woman at lunch in the kibbutz dining hall.

My mother died of cancer when she was fifty-two. She also grew up in a kibbutz, Ashdot Yaakov in the Jordan Valley. After their marriage and a short trial period in the blast furnace of the Jordan Valley, my parents moved to Ramat Yochanan, and, soon afterward, I was born.

I was born and raised on the kibbutz, the last generation that was raised in the communal living system of the children's home. Until I left the kibbutz to go to graduate school in the United States, already with a wife and baby, I spent almost my entire life in the kibbutz. At the age of fifteen, I spent a year in Holland with my family, as part of my father's work. After high school, I spent five years away from the kibbutz—one year spent in community service and another four years in the military. Yet during all that time, the kibbutz was always "home."

And now, back to the laundry list. What did we have? How can one make an accounting of the plusses and minuses of growing up on a kibbutz? The advantages and disadvantages, traumas and wonders, the good and bad, and the effect of the children's house on me and who I was to become? At first I thought to create a kind of balance sheet of what was good and what was bad. But then I changed my mind. On the dark side of kibbutz life much has already been written. On the superficial connection between the children and their parents, on the kibbutz lawnmower that didn't leave room for any individualism, and on "us" versus "me."

But why focus on the bad if you can relate what was good? Thus I decided to recount the advantages of kibbutz life from my own personal experience.

Equality among People

Ever since my studies in the United States and until today, and with my work that takes me around the world, I have had the opportunity to meet, and often befriend, many people of influence and means. My kibbutz background serves me well in these relationships, with an ability to talk with people at eye level without being intimidated or put off by their money or power. One of the more attractive values on the kibbutz of old was the equality among people. Each person, regardless of where he or she worked and how much money he had in his account, was valued. I remember there were those who carried this to an extreme, denigrating the skewed values of bourgeois city society. Kibbutz members were judged according to a different set of values: the circumference of their muscle, the size of their tractor, their rank in the army, their ability on the basketball court, and, of course, their diligence and hard work.

The Connection to the Land

In today's industrialized Western world, many people grow up without knowing what bread is made of, from where milk comes, and what is the connection between a flower and fruit. Growing up where the milk came straight from the dairy, the birth of a calf was a social occasion, the prayer for rain was accompanied by a plea that the rain would not fall before the cotton was harvested, and where the season's fruit was picked from the trees—all these taught us about the circle of life. In my youth I knew every fruit tree in every kibbutz garden. There was an undercover contest among the kids of the kibbutz over who would be the first to pick a new fruit (guava, figs, pomegranates, fijoya, persimmon, and more) even before it was entirely ripe but before anyone else got to it. When we wanted a nut cake, my mother would send us out to collect pecans from under the tree and crack them over a newspaper. Cheesecake with berries was prepared during mulberry season, picked from the mulberry tree by the school. The connection among the land, the tree, and the fruit was second nature to us.

The Work Ethic

There was no greater insult in the kibbutz society I grew up in than to call a member "lazy." It was no coincidence that the Zionist pioneers of the early twentieth century established the concept of "the religion of labor." Many violations were overlooked at the kibbutz, including several of the ground rules of moral behavior described in the Ten Commandments. But for idleness, there was no forgiveness. Naturally, hard work and dedication to one's job were highly esteemed. As if it were yesterday, I remember Zvi and Abram'ke appearing at the orchard for an early morning cup of coffee before work, proud and determined workers already well into their seventies. Once, kibbutz members insisted on working as long as they could stand on their feet. And those who didn't work? They were never forgotten. About one senior kibbutz member who reached the age of ninety after a life-long career in public service, malicious gossipers attributed his longevity to a life spent slacking off.

From a very young age, we worked. We milked goats before school, picked oranges and lemons after school, rounded up poultry at night, and the list goes on. Half of every school vacation day was allocated for work. Whoever grew up in a kibbutz learned from a young age that work was an inseparable part of life.

Independence and the Ability to Land on One's Feet

At the kibbutz I grew up in, there was no place to escape and nowhere to hide. We grew up in the company of ten other children in our same age group, living in a children's house without our parents, dependent on the grace of an intercom and the night guardswoman when we woke up from a bad dream or wet the bed. We had to prove ourselves in the agricultural field and the sports field and survive the struggles for power between children. After all that, we grew up empowered with endurance and independence, having learned to either sink or swim.

The Connection to Nature and the Seasons

From its earliest days, the Kibbutz Movement rejected and distanced religion and religious holidays. In its place, the kibbutz pioneers developed a religion of the land and of nature. Traditional holidays like Passover, Sukkot, Simchat Torah, and Rosh Hashana shifted to the agricultural and cultural. When the fall winds began to blow, driving away the summer heat, we knew that Rosh Hashana was near. And when the air filled with the intoxicating scent of the flowering citrus trees, every kibbutz member knew that Passover was around the corner. The connection among nature, agriculture, and the seasons was completely ingrained in us. Nature wasn't some abstract idea that one reads about in poetry books or sees in films. It oriented us in our world.

In the fall of 1994, I left the kibbutz, together with my wife and our eldest child, who was then six months old, a few thousand dollars saved from my army service, and plenty of motivation and "chutzpa." I had been accepted to graduate school at Harvard University in Boston. The kibbutz members asked me if that wasn't too daring a step, and I thought to myself how hard it was to see the kibbutz going capitalist. If I was going to live in a capitalist society, I might as well do it at Harvard.

One freezing Boston night, I was the first to arrive for an evening class. The classroom was dark, and, when I turned on the light, someone suddenly jumped out from under one of the desks—a homeless man with long hair and ragged clothes. Standing there face to face, we were both startled and a little frightened. He recovered first and asked, "Where did **you** come from?" "Israel," I told him. "Then welcome to America," he responded with a broad grin.

That same welcome I received from a homeless man at Harvard stays with me to this day and keeps me conscious of the balance of assets and liabilities ingrained in me from the kibbutz.

August 2010

FREEDOM OF THE SPIRIT

The human spirit is stronger than the body. This was proven to me on a recent spring day during the Tel Aviv Marathon. I came to cheer on my wife, Betsy, who had joined some eighteen thousand other runners and was taking on the half-marathon, twenty-one kilometers. Over the course of two hours, as I waited for her, I chatted with other bystanders, wandered around the various booths selling sports accessories, and relaxed on a bench on the new boardwalk of Tel Aviv Port, reading the weekend newspaper and trying not to let the news dampen my mood. Generally, people in Israel who want to maintain their good spirits should stick to reading historical and spiritual books and stay away from newspapers.

As the time approached for Betsy to reach the final stretch, I slowly made my way to the finish line. Finally, I spotted her among the thousands of other runners, stretching and releasing their muscles and sharing their impressions with their friends and families. Betsy was full of energy and spirit, and it seemed to me that she could have turned around and run the whole race again. But, instead, we went to meet another couple, friends who live in Tel Aviv, for brunch. And then we saw her.

She was seated in a special wheelchair adapted for running. She wasn't the only person in a wheelchair who participated in the marathon. More and more people with physical disabilities in Israel are joining in sports events. But then she propelled her wheelchair in our direction. She was approaching a raised median strip that separated the two lanes of the street that she was clearly intending to cross. We were about five meters away from her. There were crowds of people around her, any one of whom she could have asked for assistance. "Watch," I whispered to my wife, as I realized what this young woman was about to do. Pulling herself up out of her chair and using her hands, she climbed up onto the raised dividing strip. Then this incredible sportswoman pulled her wheelchair up beside her and sat down in it. It seemed pretty clear that she didn't want any assistance, but, still, my wife approached a group of police and asked them to check with her and see if she needed anything. But before the police officer even reached her, she'd already made her way to the other side of the road and, using the same system, continued on her way.

That anonymous woman made a strong impression on me. I don't know who she is, what her name is, where she's from, or what she does. I managed to take a picture of her from the back, thinking that I had to tell my children about her. During Shabbat, I related our encounter with this remarkable woman, and after it was over, I showed them the picture. And the next day, in karate practice, I told my students about the woman in the wheelchair.

Our bodies concern us all the time. Particularly when something doesn't function as it should—if it's pain, a wound, a cough, or just a pulled muscle—we are constantly reminded of this infraction on our physical wellbeing. In the blessing "Who Created," we express gratitude for our intact bodily functions, in all their miraculous complexity, lest we take their existence for granted.

The fascinating encounter from afar with that anonymous sportswoman is deeply etched into my consciousness. It affirmed for me the strength and determination of the spirit to overcome physical challenges as a triumphant expression of personal freedom. And these expressions of freedom, beyond the sphere of the body, must also be appreciated. Because even though they seem to us so obvious, can we imagine not having the freedom to choose our leaders, the freedom to travel, the freedom to work, the freedom to establish a family, just to name a few?

In a conversation with my friend Betsy Stern, who lives in the United States, we ran through a not so short list of reasons for concern. Looming high on that list was Israel's enemies who, as in most of the history of the Jewish people, look like they are preparing to finish us off. At the end of the conversation, I proposed to Betsy that we should also look at the full half of the cup: in all the years of Jewish history, throughout all the generations, our situation has never been better than it is these days, Erev Pesach Taf Shin Ayin Aleph. Perhaps tomorrow will be worse. But it is also important to acknowledge and appreciate today.

With the Passover holiday, holiday of freedom, approaching, we can wish for each other that we strive and succeed to express our freedom, physical and spiritual, for ourselves, our communities, and our nation.

Happy holiday!

April 2011

STRUDEL DOESN'T CROSS BORDERS

Switzerland is a country with majestic landscapes, tourist attractions, an abundance of natural treasures and resources, including what seems to be an endless amount of water, flowing and pooling at every corner. When you arrive in Switzerland from Israel, where every shower or watering of the garden can lead to a crisis of conscience, there is no greater pleasure than a long, hot shower in a hotel, knowing that the Rhine River is flowing torrentially through the center of town and that water problems are sometimes only regional. When visiting Switzerland, you start to wonder if Moses, when he was leading the Israelites out of slavery in Egypt to the Promised Land, wasn't actually wishing to reach Switzerland.

In honor of our twentieth wedding anniversary, Betsy and I went for a bicycle trip in Switzerland. Over three straight days we happily pedaled 160 kilometers along a stretch of the Rhine River. Our route passed over the borders of three countries: Switzerland, Austria, and Lichtenstein. Crossing a border in Western Europe in the twenty-first century is practically a non-event, at least for the casual tourist. One moment you're in one country, and the next moment you're in its neighbor.

One of my greatest weaknesses since childhood is apple strudel. Evidently, this can be traced to the oven of my late mother, Zehava, whose golden, fragrant apple strudel was my desire. During apple season, and at every holiday, celebration, or birthday, I was treated to one of these exceptional confections, which, after emerging from the oven, would last only twenty-four hours in the refrigerator before quickly disappearing, slice by slice, roll by roll.

When I married Betsy, she quickly recognized the magic power of strudel over her new husband, and since then she faithfully and lovingly carries on the family strudel tradition.

So when we decided to do a bicycle trip in Switzerland, knowing that it borders both Germany and Austria, the kingdoms of the strudel, it was absolutely clear to me that, between the kilometers of strenuous biking, I would be able to treat myself to the original European strudel on its home turf. My hopes for apple strudel were stellar, but they quickly came down to earth. As great as my hopes were, so was the disappointment.

From the first moment we landed in the Zurich airport, through the various train stations, and every welcoming, picturesque village that we passed through during our bicycle vacation, I asked over and over again, in my faltering German, at first out of curiosity in an assured voice full of expectancy, which would gradually trail off as the hope faded, "Do you have any apple strudel?"

To my surprise and great disappointment, the answer I received again and again was no. I tried to figure out what the root of the problem was. Why can't you find a good strudel in Switzerland?

STRUDEL DOESN'T CROSS BORDERS

At one point, Betsy and I speculated that there was no strudel because the apple season hadn't started, but then we remembered that we'd seen plenty of apples everywhere. There were also bakeries on every corner, displaying many other different kinds of cakes on their burgeoning shelves. Just apple strudel was missing!

We got the answer to the mystery toward the end of our trip, from an unexpected source in the Walzenhausen Hotel in a small village of the same name. The village of Walzenhausen is situated at the slopes of a mountain range that towers over the Rhine River and overlooks Lake Constanz, at the point where the river joins the lake on the Swiss side. It's a small village, with only about two thousand residents, and we reached it with our bicycles on a small red lift that climbed the mountain for exactly eight minutes and deposited its passengers at the front door of a beautiful spa hotel, whose restaurants and windows offered a breathtaking view of the lake and its surroundings.

We reached this delightful hotel after a tiring day of biking, sweaty, and aching. After a quick dip in the pool and the long, hot (and guilt-free) shower, we understood that the hotel restaurant was the only place in this little village where one could eat dinner. We sat down at a small table that looked out onto the exceptional view, and we ordered steamed asparagus and rice. Food is extremely costly in Switzerland, and already from the beginning of our trip we realized that paying too much attention to the prices on the menu is not advisable as it can lead to a stomachache even before the meal.

During our dinner, the hotel manager came to our table. A European gentleman, meticulously dressed and comfortably self-assured, he introduced himself, and we exchanged pleasant small talk. When he heard that we were celebrating our twentieth anniversary, he explained with a small smile that he has two wives, his beloved spouse and his hotel, and the hotel comes first. As we chatted, we found that he was very familiar with Israel and that in the past he had managed a hotel in Africa with an Israeli owner. I asked him the question that had been bothering me for days: "Why can't I find apple strudel in Switzerland?" The hotel manager smiled and explained what to him was clear and evident. "Strudel is an Austrian dish. We are Swiss. Why would we Swiss make an Austrian cake? Whoever wants Austrian strudel should go to Austria!"

And then it was clear. We weren't just talking about cake. It was a matter of national identity and patriotic pride.

I thanked the hotel manager, and he continued on to another table of guests, while I looked at my wife with satisfaction that only grew as I continued to ponder the subject. Finally, we had found a place and topic that we Israelis could relate to with satisfaction with our lot. Here in peaceful, picturesque Europe, the citizens and tourists—because of honor and national pride—must do without the most significant and important things such as apple strudel. And for us in the Middle East, the traditional foods cross man-made borders freely.

Hummus, falafel, pita bread, and baklava. These are only a few from a long list of foods that extend across borders that visiting tourists can find in Israel but also in restaurants and bakeries in the neighboring countries of Egypt, Jordan, Lebanon, and Syria.

Disagreements and conflicts we have aplenty. And water in dire shortage. Our rivers are barely streams. The borders are marked by fences and landmines, and to pass from Israel to a neighboring country is difficult and not open to everyone, but at least the food can cross freely. All hope isn't lost!

June 2011

FROM BERLIN TO MTV

To mark our twentieth anniversary, Betsy and I decided to take a bicycle tour along the Rhine, where we could enjoy our love of nature amidst the spectacular scenery of Switzerland. Every morning we left our bags at the reception desk of the hotel where we had stayed the night before and set off for a ride of about sixty kilometers along a paved bicycle path. Sometime in the afternoon we would reach our next hotel, where we would find our luggage waiting for us.

After one particularly long and enjoyable day biking along the river, we reached the small village of Buchs, located on the border between Switzerland and Lichtenstein. Exhausted, we dragged ourselves up the spiral staircase to our hotel room, intending to wash off the sweat of the day and freshen up before heading out for dinner.

In the hotel room we had a delightful surprise: a basket overflowing with fancy Swiss chocolate pralines and a charming anniversary card from the warm and welcoming hotel owner. After a long, hot shower to ease our cramped muscles, we relaxed on the bed and fed each other pralines. Betsy picked up the TV remote and started flipping through the channels, trying to find one in English.

We have not had a TV in the house since our oldest child was born because we believe children are exposed to enough garbage even without a TV. But childhood habits are hard to break; my wife grew up in America when TV was the primary household entertainment, and flipping through TV channels is a childhood bug of hers.

Europe has plenty of beautiful and interesting things for an English-speaking tourist to enjoy. Television, however, is not one of them. The vast majority of the programs are dubbed in the local language, and, in Switzerland, even Tom Cruise and Angelina Jolie talk in German.

For lack of a more interesting channel, Betsy ended up at MTV. "I know that woman!" cried Betsy excitedly, spotting a heavily made-up woman being interviewed about the sixteenth birthday party she was planning for her daughter. I will not go into the details of this idiotic program, except to say: a) the effort and expense going into the party exceeded what is required for a fancy wedding and included a new BMW for the birthday girl, and b) I thank God that my four children cannot watch such foolish programs at our house, and that young girls like that sixteen-year-old are not role models among their friends at Hoshaya.

Hunger finally overcame tiredness, so we turned off the TV and set out to find somewhere in the small village to have dinner. After checking the menus of the few restaurants in the vicinity, we settled on Tauber, a clean, picturesque restaurant on the main street.

We were the first guests of the evening and sat ourselves down at a heavy wooden table in the corner of the restaurant. The waitress told us, most politely, that they would not be opening for another ten minutes, but she let us stay seated in the meantime, so I asked her to recommend a local beer.

She brought me the beer and then, because we were the only ones in the restaurant, began to chat with us. We learned she was forty, with no children, originally from the former East Germany, and had come to Switzerland three years earlier from Berlin. In response to my questions, which gradually became more and more nosy thanks to the beer and my own curiosity, she told us that she had come here because she had fallen in love with a local farmer, whom she had met in Berlin. Blinded by love, she left the busy and vibrant city of Berlin for a small farm on a Swiss mountaintop. Unfortunately, after a year on the farm she realized she could not adapt to the monotonous village life in which conversation was mostly with cows and sheep.

I told her I came from a kibbutz in Israel, and I was sure one could find similarities between the kibbutz and the socialist East Germany. "Not at all," she answered firmly. "You could leave the kibbutz, but we couldn't leave East Germany." After she told us she had predicted the fall of the Berlin Wall when she was nineteen, I asked her, "What was it like living in East Germany?" I expected another negative answer, but I was wrong.

"I'm glad I got to grow up in East Germany, and I'm proud of the education I got," she answered. "We were educated with an ideology; we understood the importance of the group, of working toward a common goal, of achievements in sport and science. We were educated with values, not like today's youth in the West;

for them, everything revolves around money and material things. They don't have any values at all."

She said this firmly and decisively, but I detected a touch of sadness and bitterness in her strong words. I was reminded of my childhood on the kibbutz. We, too, were raised with ideals. Over time, some of those ideals proved to be unreasonable, and some of our educators did not necessarily live by those values themselves. Nevertheless, values were an intrinsic part of how we were raised.

Educating without values is very difficult. When we compare the socialism of the Israeli kibbutz, or even of East Germany, with the hedonistic, materialistic worldview of MTV, we might find that socialism still has something to teach us.

When we got up to pay and say goodbye to our former-socialist waitress, I asked if I could take her photograph and use it to illustrate her story in one of my columns. "Absolutely not!" she snapped. I was a bit taken aback by her reaction. She made me think of a thriller I had just read about the secret police in Stalinist Russia. Instinctively I glanced around, looking for secret agents and bugs. Then I realized that despite the passage of time and the fall of the Berlin Wall, despite the fact that we were in Switzerland and not East Berlin, it is hard to change the cautious habits of those who grew up in East Germany.

What was that we were saying about MTV?

June 2011

"A KING"

Eighteen years have passed since the signing of the peace agreement between Israel and the Hashemite Kingdom of Jordan. It was 1994, the year my firstborn son came into the world. For us, 1994 was a year of new beginnings and new promise.

Betsy and I watched the signing ceremony with baby Guy on our knees. Sitting with us on the couch were my mother, Zahava, and my grandfather, Michael Benartzi. In the 1930s, my maternal grandfather was one of the pioneers of Gesher and Ashdot Yaacov, kibbutzim on the border with Jordan. During my childhood visits to kibbutz Ashdot Yaacov, I was always scared of the bad people who threatened us from the mountains on the other side of the Jordan River. For me, "Jordan" was the very epitome of an enemy nation.

Inspired by watching the signing ceremony in the presence of four generations of the Benartzi-Melamed family, my wife wrote an emotional thank-you letter to then-Prime Minister Yitzhak Rabin. In her letter, Betsy thanked him for bringing the longed-for peace to Israel, and Rabin replied. In his letter, dated August 11, 1994, the late prime minister wrote: "...*it is the faces of the youth who have died never knowing peace and those who may live never knowing war which are constantly before my eyes. You wrote to me of your dreams for 5-month old Guy's future. Working together, we will turn those dreams into reality.*"

A year later, Rabin was murdered, and since then considerable water has flowed under the bridge of peace-making—much of it murky. Today, the peace agreement with Jordan is "the most peaceable" one that we have left.

The bad news is that, with the deteriorating situation in Egypt, Jordan is now essentially the only country where Israelis can cross the border as tourists. Furthermore, the economic "fruits of peace" that Israel and Jordan were expecting to tend together have, for the most part, shriveled on the vine. Of all the exciting projects that were contemplated during the last eighteen years—joint universities, amusement parks along the Jordan River, joint industrial parks, and the like—the only one that is still extant is the QIZ program: qualifying industrial zones in Jordan, employing thousands of Jordanians and producing goods that can directly access US markets without paying tariffs—provided that the goods include a certain percentage of Israeli input.

The good news is that it is still possible to cross the Jordanian border, economic and security cooperation still continues, the eastern border of Israel still requires very few IDF forces to patrol it…and an Israeli father can still take his son there for a five-day father-son trip.

Many years ago I promised Guy that when he got his black belt in karate, I would take him to Paris to train with our French *sensei*. Several years later, the time came for me to fulfill that promise.

This past year has been one of cataclysmic, earth-shattering changes in the Middle East, changes that have undermined the foundations of long-standing regimes. "Guy," I said, "Paris will still be there to welcome us if we wait another few years, but who knows how much longer we'll be able to visit Jordan? Let's go there instead."

So that is what we did. I asked my Jordanian friend Abu Rabi'a (a pseudonym) to recommend a personal guide, we planned an itinerary that would take us south of Amman via Petra and on to Wadi Ram, we made certain we did not take any items of clothing with Hebrew writing on them, and we set off to tour Jordan during the week of the Purim holiday.

In 2011, gigantic signs announcing upgrade projects popped up along the sides of Israeli highways the length and breadth of Israel. Each sign included the deadline for completion of the specific ambitious transportation project, as well as the signatures of Prime Minister Benjamin Netanyahu and Minister of Transport Yisrael Katz. One does not need to be an expert in political communication to understand that our politicians have found a creative method of getting long-term free publicity in prime locations. After all, a target date of 2014 guarantees the sign a lifetime that, in Israeli political terms, is practically an eternity. We have been lucky to have a responsible and brave public servant who managed to get these irritating advertisements removed from our roads.

We were reminded of these obtrusive highway signs during our visit to the Kingdom of Jordan, and we came to the conclusion that they represented the deep, dark secret of many Israeli politicians—perhaps, in their heart of hearts, leaders of the only democracy in the Middle East dream of being kings. We came to this conclusion because on every corner in Jordan, on every wall, on the bus, in shops, in hotels—in fact, everywhere—are displayed photographs of King Abdullah, his wife, Ranya, and earlier heads of the Hashemite royal family. The details of the various pictures of the king depended upon the location and the desired message: he might be wearing a suit, traditional Bedouin clothing, or Jordanian army uniform and standing next to a helicopter gunship, or be with his family, and so on.

The primary messages that the pictures gave were: the king takes care of the people; the king is ours; the king and the Jordanian people are one. Even after several days touring around Jordan, it was hard not to be impressed—and even be influenced—by these messages. We were reminded of King Abdullah's father, the late King Hussein. I visited Jordan the first time about twelve years ago, a few weeks after King Hussein died of cancer. It was not Jordan alone that sank into mourning; Israel did too. Israel considered King Hussein to be the most "king-like" in the region: elegant, noble, trustworthy, his beautiful wife, Noor, at his side. He won Israel's heart on a number of occasions, the most memorable of which took place under tragic circumstances. After the attack at the joint Israeli-Jordanian tourist site of Naharayim in 1997, when a Jordanian soldier shot to death seven high school girls from Beit Shemesh, King Hussein flew his helicopter to Israel, and, on his knees, gave his apologies on behalf of himself and of the Jordanian people to each bereaved family.

I have not the slightest shadow of doubt that although democracy is a problematic and inefficient form of government, it is also the best and fairest. But perhaps sometimes, just a little bit, in our heart of hearts, we might, like the Israelites in the days of Samuel the Prophet, crave for ourselves a king.

March 2012

OCCUPY...

Israel is well known as a world leader of technological, agricultural, and medical innovations. This summer, one more innovation with global implications was added to the list of Israeli creations: social protest tent camps. About six months after the tent protests on Rothschild Boulevard in Tel Aviv and the streets of other Israeli towns, the Occupy movement began to organize similar protest camps in major cities in the West.

On my last trip to North America, I visited three of these protest camps.

In Montreal, I asked my friend David Lyons to introduce me to the renowned Montreal bagels. The profile of Montreal bagels was raised internationally when a Canadian astronaut included them on his list of must-have items to take into space. The tourist brochure in my Montreal hotel room credits the bagel to our people, noting that they were brought to the country by Eastern European Jews who immigrated to Canada. I purchased half a dozen sweet bagels hot out of the oven and duly added myself to the list of their fans.

At David's suggestion, we drove from the bakery to our dinner spot via the Occupy Montreal protest camp, where we saw a few dozen colorful tents pitched along a narrow boulevard. David and I, comfortably seated in the warmth of David's car, decided that the freezing Canadian winter presents a significant challenge to the Montreal protesters' commitment to social revolution.

The next day, I arrived in Cambridge and checked into my hotel in Harvard Square, next to Harvard University, since I planned to go to Shabbat services and take my Shabbat meals at the local Hillel chapter. Not many students remained on campus that weekend. Most of them had gone to the Yale versus Harvard football game held at Yale.

Just before the entrance of Shabbat, I left the hotel and went for a walk along the paths of the university. The aristocratic red-brick buildings and proud white-framed windows of Harvard cover most of Cambridge Square. Against the background of the blue sky and the red leaves that characterize New England in autumn, Harvard University, with its permanent endowment fund of some $18 billion, radiates the power and self-confidence befitting a member of the top tier of the academic world.

I walked to Harvard Yard, intending to enter it via the gate near the Gato Rojo Café. When I was a student I used to spend considerable amount of time in that café, which is run by students and boasts the lowest coffee prices on campus. At the entrance to the yard stood a tall, intimidating police officer. "Only students with a valid student ID can enter the yard," he growled at me. I was taken aback. Harvard Yard is one of the local tourist attractions, and access to the yard had never been restricted to just students. On the contrary, one could always see dozens of tourists armed with cameras wandering around the yard.

"What happened?" I asked, my Israeli imagination running wild with thoughts of terrorism, suicide bombings, and the like. The police officer ignored my question, but I heard someone else mutter, "Protest camp." Understanding began to dawn, and my determination to go into the yard grew.

I approached the police officer again and said, as politely as I could, "I don't have student ID, but I am an alumnus of Harvard. I came from halfway around the world to see the university where I studied fifteen years ago." This piqued the curiosity of the guardian of law and order.

"Really? Where are you from?" he asked. Looking at him with his dark sunglasses, I thought he seemed to be ex-military.

"From Israel," I replied.

"You don't have an Israeli accent," declared the police officer with surprise.

"I lived in Boston for several years, so I have a 'Boston-Israeli' accent."

"Did you serve in the Israeli army?"

"Of course!" I answered proudly. "In fact, I still serve, as a captain in the reserves."

My military service and rank worked its magic on the police officer. "Okay, I'll give you a break, officer to officer. You can go into the yard."

I thanked him and went straight in before he could change his mind. I headed for the protest tents, which were pitched atop a manicured lawn, just a few yards from the famous statue of John

Harvard. Harvard bequeathed his extensive library and about half of his monetary estate to the academic institution then known as the New College, in appreciation for which America's oldest and most prestigious university has, since 1639, been named for him.

The Occupy Harvard camp consisted of about twenty tents, next to which was a small table with explanatory brochures. I asked the bearded young man at the table to tell me the purpose of the protest. His name was Timothy McGraff, and he was a doctoral student in American history.

"Harvard must use its international influence to make the world a fairer place," Timothy said and told me to visit the Occupy Harvard movement's website, *www.occupyharvard.net*, for more information. "It's not good enough that Harvard leads the business, public, and academic worlds. We must use our influence in the world to make it a better place." The future PhD and present-day revolutionary agreed with me that the name "Occupy" is very threatening and intimidating. "You're right," he said. "The name 'We are the ninety-nine percent' sounds much better." Despite the paucity of tents and the university administration's policing efforts, I left the camp feeling that something significant might be happening there.

When Shabbat exited, I joined my friends Larry and Elaine Smith for dinner. After supper, Larry suggested that we go to see the Occupy Boston camp. We walked to the camp, which consisted of over one hundred tents organized in rows that reminded me of the tent camp on Rothschild Boulevard. On the corner of the boulevard were a central kitchen, a library, and an information tent. Banners were raised 'protesting against' various evils and 'protesting for' various remedies. Bundled up in warm clothing, some of the activists were explaining their doctrine to passersby. Boston in November is cold. It is not easy to be a revolutionary in a pup tent when the temperature drops below freezing, and winter will be a real test of the movement. We listened to one of the activists for a few minutes then the fierce cold won out over our curiosity and we walked home briskly.

Over the next few days I spoke with some of my American friends about the developing phenomenon of the Occupy movement. I learned that some of the protests have already put Israel and Jews in our traditional starring roles as the "bad guys," and those protests include slogans like, "Get rid of the Jewish bankers" or "Free occupied Palestine."

The Occupy movement is growing on fertile ground for protest. The current global economic crisis is liable to dramatically increase the numbers of educated people within the ranks of the unemployed and to further widen the large gaps between those who benefit from capitalism and those who are its victims. If the protests become radicalized and start to lead to violence and extremism then the likely results will be destructive to society as a whole—including to the weaker segments of the population that the movement was intended to help.

I will not be surprised if we soon hear convoluted conspiracy theories according to which Israel and the Jews are using their secret weapon, developed by Daphni Leef and her colleagues and tested during the social protest movement in Israel, to disrupt the entire global economy via the Occupy movement. Unfortunately, when troubles and catastrophes plague the world, there are always those who blame everything on the Jews.

But what if the protest movement leads to good things? If that happens, will the world remember that the social protest movement was born in Israel, on Rothschild Boulevard, in the summer of 2011?

November 2011

YES, SHE CAN!

From my office window, I looked out over the fields of the Yezreel Valley, extending north to the hills of Nazareth and adorned with the first tentative green of the approaching winter. The student I shall call "Ahlaam" stopped talking. She took a paper tissue from the box I offered her and wiped away her tears. "Noor," sitting next to Ahlaam and holding her one-year-old on her lap, smiled adoringly at Ahlaam.

Ahlaam is a first-year student in the department of management information systems at Yezreel Valley College. Her personal story, which she was telling me in the context of my work at the college, touched my heart, representing as it does the struggle that Israeli Arab women have with the limitations imposed on them by tradition and convention.

Ahlaam is about thirty years old. She was born in one of the largest Arab cities in Israel to a very religious family. At a young age she rebelled against the traditional lifestyle of her family. In high school she excelled, and her grade-point average in her matriculation exams was over one hundred. She always dreamed of studying computers and joining the high-tech industry.

After Ahlaam finished high school, she was unable to fund post-secondary studies and did not receive any support for her ambitions from her family, so she had to make do with working as a junior clerk, earning a monthly salary of about two to three thousand NIS (about seven or eight hundred dollars). I wondered aloud whether such a low salary was even legal, being far below Israel's minimum wage. "That's the reality we Arab women live with," Ahlaam muttered bitterly. "My employer said if I didn't like it, he could find a thousand other women who would be delighted to swap places with me." Noor nodded in agreement.

A few years ago Ahlaam got married and hoped that with the support of her educated husband she could fulfill her dream and take a degree in computer science. Her hopes were dashed. When she registered at the college, she found out that her husband objected to her going for a degree. "It would change the current balance of power where he is the one who is educated and who brings home the better salary, and he was threatened by that. He wants me at home taking care of our children and his elderly parents. In his view, a woman's place is in the home, not in academia or industry." Her eyes became glazed with tears, and I felt she was revealing more than she had intended to. I apologized and told her that she did not have to tell me anything more.

But Ahlaam clearly felt the need to unburden herself, and she continued talking. "Not only does he expect me to take care of the house and children; he also expects me to take care of his parents. Everyone is watching me, waiting for me to fail, for me not to be able to combine college studies and also function as a perfect wife, mother, homemaker, and daughter-in-law. But I am determined to succeed despite his opposition and the obstacles he raises. I took a loan from the bank to finance my studies, and I know I can do it."

Ahlaam's story is not unusual. A young Muslim Arab woman who wants to get an education and become part of the Israeli workforce has to deal with several challenges:

The challenge of integrating into the mainstream of Israeli society. While it is true that several major companies in Israel are becoming increasingly geared up to integrate minority populations (including the ultra-Orthodox) into their workforces, and although both the Israeli government and social organizations have taken many concrete steps toward this goal, it is still much harder for Arabs to integrate into the Israeli workforce than for their Jewish neighbors.

Within Arab society, in particular the Muslim sector, women have to deal with an extremely low glass ceiling. The responsibilities for running the household, taking care of the children, and caring for parents—the husband's parents as well as the wife's—all fall on the women. In most Arab families, the husband never sets foot in the kitchen, does not wash the floors, and would never dream of changing a diaper. In addition, from the religious perspective of "woman's modesty," it is not very acceptable for a woman to work freely alongside men.

In the Galilee and other areas on the "periphery" of Israel, employment opportunities are far more limited than they are in the center of the country. Competition for work is so intense that there are many applicants for every available job, and Arab women start out at a great disadvantage.

One cannot overstate the importance of creating opportunities for Arab women like Ahlaam to acquire an education and become part of advanced industries. There would be several benefits to the country in general and to the periphery in particular:

One: Adding ambitious and skilled employees to the employment pool and increasing the percentage of the population that participates in the workforce

Two: Increasing the supply of trained personnel for advanced industries in the periphery, encouraging companies to expand their activities to areas that suffer from lack of skilled employees

Three: Creating additional income for households, thus increasing the amount available for discretionary expenditures and increasing economic activity in the periphery

Four: Strengthening modernizing trends in the Arab sector and its integration into mainstream Israeli society and weakening the trend toward extremism and sectarianism

Five: Creating a more just society

Make no mistake, the revolution is already here. More and more young Arab men and women are getting an education, realizing their ambition to become part of the advanced industries of Israel. Increasing numbers of pioneering companies are identifying and employing this educated and ambitious population. Israel is investing more resources and efforts to support this trend. But the fact that such companies are still considered unusual shows that this great potential is currently leveraged only to a very small extent.

To Ahlaam and the thousands of other women who are fighting to break through the glass ceiling, you can do it! I wish you every success!

December 2011

DIRT

In recent years I have noticed that I find hiking along Israel's nature trails less and less enjoyable. Hiking around Israel had been one of my favorite hobbies. When I was a teen, I wrote on my backpack, "For your feet will know the land," and there were very few streams, mountains, or valleys that I had not hiked.

When I first noticed my diminishing pleasure in hiking, I explained it away as an inevitable part of the aging process—the years go by, and the legs and back are no longer what they used to be. That is part of the story, of course, but I think there is another reason: the frustration and depression that assail me each time I encounter the dirtiness of the country.

Why, on this little stretch of land where Abraham settled, where Jesus was born, where Mohammed visited, a country that has produced Nobel Prize winners, an advanced army, and excellent universities, a place whose primary resources are brainpower and determination, whose territory is so tiny and every square inch of which is precious—why, oh, why did such a special country, blessed with an extraordinary history and extraordinary capabilities, become so littered?

I used to think it bothered me so much because this is **my** country, the land where I was born and raised, so I am hyper-sensitive to its dirt and pollution. Then I began to take note of every other country I visited, and my frustration simply grew. Of course, for countries such as Switzerland and Canada we can still use the tired old argument, "They don't have our security problems. If our borders were as quiet as Switzerland's, we would be as clean as Switzerland." But the last straw for me was my visit to Slovenia, a country that only came into existence about two decades ago and where they still plough the fields using horses in some of their villages. Betsy and I travelled through Slovenia for a week and never once saw litter. In the beginning we thought we had simply chanced upon a particularly clean village or a well-managed city with a good mayor, but in the end we realized that the entire country was simply…clean.

In Israel, there have been many attempts and much effort invested in trying to keep the country clean. This is not a new problem, and public awareness is, ironically, improving. We now have a Ministry of the Environment, various public organizations are active in the field, tourist sites are turned into national parks with entrance fees, recycling and trash collection are becoming more efficient all the time. But despite all this, our country is still dirty.

Why?

I *Googled* the phrase "Why is Israel dirty?" and what I found was fascinating. The top-ranked results did not talk about physical dirt at all but about metaphorical "dirt"—Israel's standing in the world:

"'Israel' is a dirty word" (a quote from Obama's personal pastor).

"Israel's dirty secret in Gaza"

Since Google did not give me a satisfactory answer, I tried to analyze the phenomenon myself and had the following thoughts:

Perhaps this has to do with a **feeling of transience**. One morning, as I was sitting on my balcony at home, I looked out over the neighboring Tzipori National Park. I asked myself, "How did the residents of Tzipori take care of their environment thousands of years ago? Did their attitude toward the cleanliness of the country differ from that of people in our age?"

We all know that most people do not take as good care of a room in a motel or temporary residence as they do of their own homes. The Jewish people have wandered around the world for thousands of years—the term "The Wandering Jew" was coined for a good reason. Has there ever been a serious, in-depth discussion about how Israel will look in the year 2050? If the subject ever comes up, it is only in the context of the possible demographic threat. Perhaps we still feel like temporary residents. Perhaps that is the reason we are less committed than we should be to keeping the place squeaky-clean.

Perhaps we still **have the feeling of being hounded and persecuted.** Life feels short and fleeting, so we have the attitude, "Eat, drink, and be merry, for tomorrow we may die." Faced as we are with constant, unrelenting threats to our very existence, long-term planning may seem out of place. Perhaps this is what is preventing us from making the necessary commitment to keeping our country clean.

The **sense of belonging** is another factor, influencing both the community and the individual. During the winter I swim in a swimming pool in Nazareth. When I drive from my home in Hoshaya to the swimming pool, I pass the Arab village of Illut. The road into the village is a depressing sight. It looks more like a garbage dump than a thoroughfare, with piles of building waste, bottles, tires, animal carcasses, and other trash lining the sides of the road.

Is there a relationship between extreme filth and the fact that sometimes the residents have to pass police barricades on the way to the village, that the village has been the scene of struggles between the police and organized crime? Is it fair to conclude that in minority communities and in neighborhoods characterized by low socio-economic populations, keeping the area clean is not a high priority for the residents?

I cannot pretend to offer solutions. Many others, far smarter and more experienced than I, have tried to offer solutions to no avail. Instead, I will offer two ideas:

First, perhaps the time has come to promote an Israeli sense of shame. After four generations of repressing the quintessential Jewish guilt complex and instead celebrating our Sabra chutzpah, bluntness, and ability to improvise, perhaps the time has come to start respecting the feeling of shame. I believe we would be better off if Israelis were ashamed to throw trash out their car windows, ashamed to drop trash on the nature trails, ashamed to leave behind litter at picnic sites.

Second, I believe we must not despair. We have no other country; we cannot go down to the local agora and trade it in for another. The struggle to keep our country clean is difficult, exhausting, and very frustrating for those at the forefront of the efforts. But there is no alternative. This campaign bears many resemblances to the movement to reduce traffic accidents. It is almost a holy campaign. Throwing up our hands and resigning ourselves to the current situation means giving up our rights and our future in this country.

October 2011

AND SHOW DEFERENCE

"Program '15 Yehezkel Street, Jerusalem' into your GPS, and we'll meet at Pessach's home [fictitious name and address]. He'll take us on a tour of the Chanukah menorahs in the ultra-orthodox neighborhood of Mea Shearim. It'll be very interesting," said our friend Eran Rolls, calling us on the third night of Chanukah. Eran was right; the visit turned out to be very interesting indeed.

We got to Jerusalem about half an hour ahead of the Rolls family. Pessach's apartment looked as if it had been transported from a little nineteenth-century Jewish town. The walls had no windows and instead were covered by shelves crammed with religious books, and the main room was decorated with pictures of rabbis. The little children were in the corner of the kitchen, eating takeout pizza out of the box. Pessach's wife was dressed from head to toe in black, and her hair was enclosed in a black head covering. She did not greet us. I later learned that it was not simply because she observes extreme rules of modesty but also because we lack a common language. "She speaks only Yiddish," explained Pessach.

Pessach dresses like a Haredi, looks like a Haredi, lives in a Haredi neighborhood, and is affiliated with the extreme ultra-orthodox *Toldot Aharon* sect, yet he showed an uncharacteristic openness to the world outside the Haredi community. As I walked into his apartment with my family, it suddenly dawned on me that I had never before sat in the living room of an ultra-orthodox Jew. I realized I had been given an opportunity, and I decided to be as open as I could, to listen carefully and to put aside my instinctive objections to many aspects of Haredi life.

At my request, Pessach described the lifestyle of his Haredi community. "An average family has about eight children. The children study ten to twelve hours a day, all religious studies except for two hours of mathematics. There are no televisions or radios and practically no computers. The only time we go on a trip is to visit the graves of holy people. I am one of the few in the community who owns a car. My wife and I got married at nineteen. It was an arranged marriage, as are all marriages here. There's almost no divorce because the reasons we get married and our expectations from marriage are different from those of the non-Haredi community. Most members of the community live very frugally, practically hand to mouth. We carefully consider every shekel and every purchase, but, with the help of *HaShem*, we get by."

I asked about violence and conflicts, since they live in such cramped conditions. "There are clashes between different ideological groups within the Haredi community. Recently there have been conflicts between the *Sicarii* [a faction considered overzealous even by the extreme *Toldot Aharon*] and the *Gur Chasidim*." He described the source of the conflict: "They're fighting over control of apartment buildings that were built over a hundred years ago by donors from Europe as cheap housing for young people." I had to smile at his description since this was clearly a very NON-ideological conflict.

By degrees I got to the difficult questions. "And what is your attitude to the State of Israel?"

"We are opposed to the existence of Israel," he answered pleasantly but firmly. "The existence of the State of Israel is delaying the redemption. We are waiting for the arrival of the Messiah, son of David. Only when the Messiah arrives can we rebuild the Holy Temple." I asked him to describe how the country would look after the Messiah arrives. His eyes sparkled with excitement, and his voice rose an octave. In my innocence I expected him to launch into a description of the prayers and the festivals or perhaps to talk about Isaiah's messianic vision of "the wolf will dwell with the lamb" (Isaiah 11:6). But instead he began to paint a portrait of the animal sacrifices that would be offered up in the Third Temple. As he warmed to his subject, I began to worry that his detailed description of the sacrificial process would make my whole family vegetarians.

Out of respect for my host, and because I wanted to hear more of the worldview of his community, I refrained from asking Pessach the question that was threatening to burst from my lips: does he truly believe that life under Turkish, Palestinian, or Iranian rule would be better for his community and would expedite the redemption?

With the arrival of the Rolls family, we lit the Chanukah candles and went out under Pessach's guidance for a tour of the Chanukah menorahs in the Haredi neighborhood. The lit candles twinkled in the windows and doorways of the homes and gave off a soft, bright light. But it was a Thursday night, and I was distracted by the smells coming from the bakeries that were preparing *challot* bread for Shabbat. I activated the "bakery detector" in my experienced baker nose, and my younger daughter and I sniffed our way to the ultimate challah. That is the reason I was not by my wife's side when some local youths started harassing her about her "immodest dress." They must have been staring and imagining something because in fact we were all dressed in long, heavy coats due to the cold weather. The boys were lucky that Betsy was not forced to demonstrate her second Dan black belt karate skills on them.

The evening reminded me of an afternoon many years ago, in the 1970s, when we sat beside the kibbutz swimming pool with Tal Faran, the youth counselor of our junior high school class. Tal, who was only a few years older than us, watched the Swedish girls who volunteered then at the kibbutz and shared with us some of his life wisdom. "When a man's hormones don't have an outlet, they climb up his body. When they reach his eyes and brain, he stops seeing with his own eyes and stops using his brain." Tal's rather simplistic theory goes a long way to explain some of the recent incidents of bullying, humiliation, and violence toward women. Examining the fears, complexes, and frustrations of men in the Haredi community could be more useful than focusing on the modesty or lack thereof of women.

In recent weeks, the word "*hadara*" has been appearing frequently in the Israeli media. I had always considered "*hadara*" to refer to respect and deference, to honoring the wise and the elderly, as it says in the Torah (Leviticus 19:32): "Stand up in the presence of the elderly, and show deference ('*ve-hadarta*') to the old, and be God-fearing." However, the recent public discourse has been concerned with a different meaning of "*hadara*": "exclusion" as in "the exclusion of women." In this sense, "*hadara*" is used to mean "to prevent" or "to distance." It would be better if the Haredi public would concern itself more with the first meaning, with respect and with being God-fearing, and less with the second meaning, excluding and degrading women.

To illustrate, I will end with a short story I found on the Internet:

"On the eve of *Sukkot* (the Tabernacles), Reb Aryeh Levin came to Meah Shearim and went into one of the shops that had changed its stock entirely for Sukkot, and instead of books it was selling sets of the *Four Species (http://www.jewfaq.org/holiday5.htm#Arba)*. Reb Aryeh Levin went into the shop and the shopkeeper gave him an *etrog* (citron). Reb Aryeh Levin did not examine the etrog at all but instead put it straight into his pocket and left the store.

"Hayim Be'er saw what had happened and was very surprised. He said to Aryeh Levin, 'Everyone here, even the youngsters, know they should check their *etrog* with a magnifying glass. Why did you just put yours in your pocket without checking it at all?"

"Reb Aryeh Levin said to him, 'In the Torah we see the word '*hadar*' twice: The first time it says '*ve-hadarta pnei zaken*' ('and show deference to the old') and the second time it says '*pri etz hadar*' ('fruit of the citrus tree'). Many people obey the second injunction and are willing to pay a lot of money for excellent, close-to-perfect *etrog*, and that is all well and good. But I have taken to heart the other verse, and I am hurrying from here to the leper hospital in Talbiya, where I will 'show deference to the old,' and I hope I will do so honestly and faithfully.'"

December 2011

THEY DON'T MAKE THIS KIND OF PEOPLE ANYMORE

I gazed with amazement at the group of senior citizen men who had gathered in the auditorium: battle-scarred, erect, sinewy, weathered complexions, and gruff. For a moment my imagination blended the shapes of these veteran fighters with the ancient olive trees I saw through the window of the auditorium.

I went over to greet my friend Shimon Kahanar (Katche), now seventy-seven years old. Katche was a member of the legendary 101 army unit. A cattleman, a pioneer, and a fighter. Even though he has lived for many more years on a cattle ranch at the top of Mount Gilboa, Katche is still known as "Katche from Kibbutz Neve Eitan." He was clearly rather embarrassed to be seen in public using a cane. "At your age and all that you have been through, Katche, you're allowed to use a cane," I said. "After all, you were injured several times during your military career, weren't you?" "More like one big injury that put me in the hospital for a year," he replied with a hesitant smile and quickly changed the subject. "But I feel fine. Everything's great."

I left Katche and went to say hello to Gedalia Gal, aged seventy-eight. Gedalia fought as a commander in all of Israel's wars up until the Yom Kippur War and is a former Member of Knesset, a member of a moshav, and still today a public figure. A year ago he underwent major surgery. Despite the operation, he said he was feeling "excellent." "My doctor complains that I won't tell him where it hurts," joked Gedalia.

These veteran fighters were assembled to mark the seventh anniversary since the death of their comrade-in-arms and commander, Rafael (Raful) Eitan. The ceremony took place at the Yezreel Valley College, near Raful's home on Moshav Tel Adashim. Time has not diminished the power of their shared experiences that were burned in their memories over the years in sweat, blood, fear, and bravery. When one of the speakers described in detail a night raid on a Jordanian army post in the '50s, during the course of which a Jordanian guard was taken out with a commando knife, I heard a collective gasp from the row of young women soldiers sitting in front of me.

"Every year fewer and fewer people attend," whispered one of the organizers. "The group is getting smaller and smaller, and even among those who are still alive, it's hard for them to get here."

But I saw something beautiful and heroic in the annual gathering of these people of the soil and the sword. What a special group they are! *They don't make this kind of people anymore*, I thought to myself.

The practical Zionist vision became a reality largely thanks to these people and people like them. Expressing emotion is not one of their "core competencies"; they have no patience for pretty speeches and high-flown rhetoric. On the contrary, when a man from the Yezreel Valley speaks for more than three minutes at a time, he will apologize to his listeners for talking too much. But whenever there were fields to plow, tractors to repair, fortresses to storm, fighters to lead, land to settle, the laconic residents of "The Valley" were always the first in line.

A couple of years ago I attended the graduation ceremony of the air force pilots' course. The announcer read the names and places of residence of each pilot cadet. I began to keep count and discovered that about 20 percent of the graduates of the course came from the Yezreel Valley. This year my son Guy, eighteen, took part in the entry exam for the Navy Seals. When he came home exhausted from the mentally and physically challenging test, he told us that there were more youngsters from the Yezreel Valley, where we live, than from the far more populous Tel Aviv area.

It has been over a century since the establishment of Merhavia, Genigar, Nahalal, Kfar Yehoshua, Ein Harod, and the rest of the communities in the valley. There seems to be something in the valley's soil, water, air, tradition—something that still, despite everything, provides fertile ground for activist Zionist education.

The massive poster in the Communications Auditorium where we were sitting for Raful's memorial displayed the motto of his life: "Farmer—Fighter—Educator."

Nowadays, when to many Israelis "farmer" means "Thai worker," "fighter" means "someone who did not manage to wriggle out of it," and "educator" means "a sucker who is willing to settle for a low-paying job," we should salute the spirit that characterizes the residents of the valley and the example of the special breed of people like Gedalia and Katche who built, defended, and led our country by example.

December 2011

MAH YIHIYEH?

Nothing is more effective for getting an Israeli to talk than asking, "*Mah yihiyeh?*" ("What will be?"). Ironically, given the loquacity that results, "*mah yihiyeh?*" is in fact a rhetorical question that means, more or less, "How is this all going to end?" "*Mah yihiyeh?*" is the key that unlocks an Israeli's pent-up traumas, hopes, fears, dreams, expectations, and disappointments. The protest movement that swept Israel during the summer of 2011 merely added certain piquancy to that question.

After a business meeting at the Hebrew University's Givat Ram campus, I waited for an Egged bus to take me to the campus's entrance. It was a clear day, and the air was heady with the scent of pine resin coming from the trees that shaded the pathways of the campus and gave it a pastoral atmosphere. For a few moments I could forget the great burden of expectations that always seem to be in the air of the Holy City of Jerusalem.

When the green Egged bus pulled up, I saw it had no other passengers. I got on and asked the driver the cost of the ticket. When he heard that I was only going the short distance to the campus entrance, he made a friendly gesture and told me there was no need to pay. "It's on the house." He smiled.

I was pleasantly surprised by the driver's flexible and generous approach. Israeli buses may not be as reliable as Swiss buses, where one can set one's watch by the bus's arrival, but such an irregular act by a Swiss bus driver would never have been countenanced.

The friendly driver was thirty years old, heavy-set, and wearing the regulation blue Egged shirt. I realized he wanted some conversation, so I smiled and asked him the question that makes every Israeli a current affairs analyst: "Mah yihiyeh?" That was all the driver needed—he opened his mouth and out spilled his frustration and bitterness.

"The situation in Israel is lousy! Everything's screwed up. If I didn't have young children I'd be out of here tomorrow. There's nothing we can do to fix it. I was in the army for three years. True, not in a combat unit, but, still, that should count for something. My wife works for the government. We both have relatively good jobs, I work extra shifts, but we still can't get by. Why should I have to pay thirty-five percent income tax on the money I get for the extra shift? How come you can't earn a decent living here? What kind of a country is this?!"

The generous driver's face was angry and bitter as he continued his frustrated monologue. I was overwhelmed with guilt, thinking I had ruined his day, and I was sorry I had asked the question.

I decided to try to make things better. When we got to the campus gates and I was about to get off, I said, "A society like ours, here in Israel, you won't find anywhere else. At least here the problems are OUR problems. At least here we can complain in Hebrew—and sometimes someone will even listen in Hebrew!"

His face softened into agreement as his perspective changed. He smiled and waved me goodbye, his mood instantly sunnier. My feeling of guilt evaporated.

So...mah yihiyeh?"

September 2011

GAM VE-GAM

A few weeks ago, Israel had general elections. Although uncertainty still reigns regarding the makeup and character of the next government of Israel, fresh winds are already blowing in the air, and there seems to be a widespread feeling among large segments of the Israeli public that something good happened here. I believe this "something good" can be summarized in two Hebrew words: *gam ve-gam*.

For the last few decades, Israeli politics have been characterized by an emphasis on differences. Extremism. Partisan politics. Using fear for electoral gain. Leveraging hatred of The Other instead of offering support, love, and acceptance of differences. Left versus right. (If you were to ask ten random people in the street to tell you the political difference between left and right, perhaps one will manage to give even a partial answer, and yet everyone throws those terms around freely.)

Gam ve-gam means "both this and that," and a *gam ve-gam* attitude is the antithesis of the typical polarization we are used to in politics. ***Gam ve-gam*** is the ability to understand both sides of an issue and to develop an approach that incorporates the good of both.

In our home we do not have a TV set. When our oldest was born nineteen years ago, we thought that having a TV was an excellent way to invite junk entertainment and commercial brainwashing into the house. Somehow or other we have managed without TV. No TV means the Israeli politicians I see are in the flesh, at conferences or events—or on "Eretz Nehederet" ("Wonderful Country"), a weekly program that satirizes current affairs and that we watch via the Internet.

It would be interesting to see some research into the effect of "Eretz Nehederet" on the attitudes of the Israeli public toward its elected officials. I would guess that it has a greater effect on the public consciousness than all the conventional election broadcasts we see leading up to an election. Sometimes the impersonators are so good that it seems as if the actual politician is merely imitating a character on a TV satire show.

The surprise success of the 2013 elections was Yair Lapid. "Eretz Nehederet" had presented him as indecisive, as someone who wants to please everyone, a nice guy who wants to satisfy every sector of the public, someone without a clear, firm stand—a politician of ***gam ve-gam***.

What does ***gam ve-gam*** mean in practice? ***Gam ve-gam*** means:

- Understanding that it is possible to be both a proud secularist and also to appreciate, respect, understand, and even enjoy the immense importance of the tradition and religion of the people of Israel. The religion of the people of Israel belongs

to all Jews and not just to those who claim to have the sole true approach and who want to put up barriers to others.
- Understanding that it is possible to zealously defend Israel's security, military superiority, and borders, to be on guard against its enemies, and at the same time to have empathy and seek a solution for the distress of another people who are living among us under occupation. Even if we ignore the opinions of others, occupying another people damages Israeli society.
- Understanding that is vital to support entrepreneurs, free market competition, and excellence, and also vital to provide a social safety net for the weaker segments of society, to help those who are not doing well—those who never had the opportunity or who simply got left behind. The problems of the weaker segments will in the long run also hurt the strong. In our start-up nation, we must never accept a situation where the homeless rummage through garbage cans to find something to eat.
- Understanding that we can maintain the Jewish character of Israel and also display inclusivity, respect, and trust toward its non-Jewish population.

At the children's karate practice at Hoshaya two days after the elections, I used Yair Lapid's Cinderella story as a way to give a quick lesson in democracy and also to encourage the children's commitment to the Japanese martial art. "You see," I said, "we finally have a politician in the Knesset who is a black belt in karate. He practiced hard and you can see where that got him. For sure his karate will help him in politics as well."

But the truth is nothing is "for sure" in Israeli politics. Even if Lapid had several black belts—in karate, judo, aikido, or even tae kwon do—it is not certain that would be enough to help the freshly minted politician. I did not vote for him, but if Lapid can prove to the Israeli public that the ***gam ve-gam*** approach is feasible, even if he starts with just a few areas, then his place in the Israeli "Hall of Fame" would be assured.

Let us all try to help ***gam ve-gam*** to succeed.

February 2013

BEING CHOSEN CARRIES OBLIGATIONS

"The customer service manager isn't in the office this morning. Call back this afternoon," said the brusque woman on the other end of the line at the central branch of one of the leading financial institutions in Israel.

"But I've been a customer of yours for thirty years. Even my *children* are your customers. Can't you leave her a message to say I phoned and ask her to call me back?"

"Sorry, we don't take messages here; that's not our policy," she snapped.

I made one last attempt. "Every time I land at Ben-Gurion Airport I see your company motto in giant letters along the walkway from the plane: 'Being the Chosen Carries Obligations!*' So shouldn't you live up to that?"

Tenafly, New Jersey. The beautiful Jewish community center of Tenafly, one of the most flourishing Jewish communities in the area. I had been invited to speak at the center as part of their one-day university program.

The title of my talk was "From Tahrir Square to Rothschild Boulevard." I started by presenting the thesis that, contrary to popular opinion, the Western world received the inspiration for the Occupy movement from the Arab Spring uprisings, a movement that began in the streets and squares of the Arab world then made a stop-over in Rothschild Boulevard in Tel Aviv and in other places in Israel before landing in the cities of North America. I then moved on to discuss various challenges currently facing Israel.

The audience was alert and involved. They challenged me with various pointed questions. One question in particular was asked several times in one form or another by various people:

Why does the world demand of Israel standards of morality that are far higher than those it demands of itself?

Why is it that when the IDF accidentally kills ten Palestinians, the world cries out in horror, but when the American army kills one hundred civilians in Afghanistan, Iraq, or Libya, that is considered just "one of those things" that happen in a war? Why do the world's media look through a magnifying glass of criticism at the actions of the Jews, who are still fighting a war of survival on an island of relative sanity and democracy in the heart of the Arab world, where they are outnumbered many times over?

Fundraising is not an easy job, to say the least. Many people have told me, "I could never ask people for donations." But one of the biggest privileges of working in fundraising is the opportunity for fascinating encounters around the world with smart, experienced, interesting people who are leaders in their fields. During working meetings in New York following my talk in Tenafly, I took the opportunity to pose the question to some of my friends in the fields of diplomacy, advertising, and investments. **Why is the Jewish state expected to be more moral than any other country in the world?**

Their answers can be summarized as follows:

The first reason is that we are called The Chosen People, as it says in our prayer book, "And you chose us from all peoples..." Both Christianity and Islam consider Judaism their precursor religion, are influenced by it, and are, to a greater or lesser extent, based on it. We were chosen by God to receive the Torah. We were the first-born. Being "chosen" is not so much a privilege and more a burden and responsibility—this "chosen-ness" is very hard to renounce. After all, we cannot say, "No, I'm not chosen!"

The second reason, and one that has always been with us, is that the world still contains Jew-hatred and bigotry against Jews, even though it often wears different faces. I will leave it to the experts to determine the roots of this bigotry, but there is no doubt that one of the causes is jealousy: jealousy of the sibling who is successful and smart—the "chosen" one. It is not by chance that the proportion of Jews among the students and faculty of the top universities in the USA is much higher than their numbers in the general population. And have we mentioned Nobel Prizes?

The third and most important reason is that it is a privilege to be the Chosen People. We should not allow our standards to drop. We should hold ourselves to the highest possible standards. Without this high expectation of ourselves, without striving to set the bar higher, to be stronger, smarter, and more ethical, we will not become the people we aspire to be.

After all: **Being Chosen Carries Obligations!**

*Slogan has been changed to maintain anonymity.

May 2012

Made in the USA
Lexington, KY
21 October 2014